Love and Marriage

Love and Marriage

Cultural Diversity in a Changing World

Serena Nanda

John Jay College of Criminal Justice

Long Grove, Illinois

For information about this book, contact:
Waveland Press, Inc.
4180 IL Route 83, Suite 101
Long Grove, IL 60047-9580
(847) 634-0081
info@waveland.com
www.waveland.com

Photo credits: 15 Monkey Business Images/Shutterstock.com; **22** windmoon/ Shutterstock.com; **27** TonyV3112/Shutterstock.com; **34** Prathmesh Kapoor; **38** sirtravelalot/Shutterstock.com; **46** Elena Odareeva/Shutterstock.com; **50** CP DC Press/Shutterstock.com; **55** Mansoreh/Shutterstock.com; **59** rigvovan/Shutterstock.com; **65** Matej Hudovernik/Shutterstock.com; **71** KiwiGraphy Studio/Shutterstock.com; **87** © The Granger Collection Ltd.; **92** © The Granger Collection Ltd.; **97** matthew stuttard/Shutterstock.com; **109** Rawpixel/Shutterstock.com; **113** Serena Nanda

10-digit ISBN 1-4786-3755-2
13-digit ISBN 978-1-4786-3755-4

Printed in the United States of America

7 6 5 4 3 2 1

Contents

Preface

I have always been captivated by the stories people tell and the diversity of human cultures. Because of this deep interest, cultural anthropology was the perfect field for me to study and teach. I feel honored that I have been able to spend my professional career spreading the word, through my writing and in the classroom, about the importance of understanding both human similarities and human differences. My interests have mainly centered on gender issues and their interaction with other aspects of a society, which is the basis of my interest in love and marriage, the central topic of this book.

My earliest research was on marriage and family in India, which introduced me to a system in great contrast to that of my own North American culture. On one of my early field trips, I met my husband, who is Indian, and this expanded both my interest and knowledge of Indian family relationships. My interest in this field deepened as I continued my research and writing aimed at both academic and general audiences. In what I consider the true spirit of cultural anthropology, each chapter of this book is based on fieldwork by anthropologists in diverse societies around the world. The book is designed for a wide range of anthropology, sociology, and psychology courses suitable for students who have little prior knowledge of social science theory or diverse cultures. Each chapter explores the emotions and practices connected to sexuality, love, marriage, gender, and family in specific cultural settings, including the United States, which is viewed as just one culture among many others. The chapters introduce both the cultural ideal and the realities of cultural patterns, and ways in which these may contrast and even conflict with each other.

In each chapter I examine the relevant cultural patterns as they are affected by global and local changes. These changes particularly include the worldwide spread of the Western idea of romantic love and companionate marriage, which is impacting cultures everywhere. Although I have tried to limit technical terms, which often impede rather than encourage our understanding of the topics described here, some technical terminology is necessary to explore the diversity of these cultural systems. A glossary of highlighted technical terms is appended. Each chapter also includes four discussion questions that will motivate student interest and serve as a basis for student essays and discussion.

It gives me the greatest pleasure to acknowledge and thank the many people who have been so important to me in the writing of this book. First among them is my husband, Ravinder Nanda, and the many members of his family that I have grown so close to over the years. Deep thanks also to Chris Orzillo, who told me to "just do it," and Joan Young, who brainstormed each of the chapters with me, and my research assistant, Paisley Gregg. Deepest thanks also to my friends and colleagues whose ideas and suggestions were so helpful in many different ways: Barbara Backer, Niko Besnier, Elvio Evangeloni, Rick Feinberg, Douglas Feldman, Adnan Hossain, Barbara Joans, Judy Joseph, Janet and Barry Kass, Hannah Lessinger, Lamont Lindstrom, Jill Norgren, and Richard Warms. I also wish to thank the very helpful librarians at John Jay College and New York University, and I am particularly grateful to an anonymous reviewer as well as Katherine Dettwyler for all their very valuable comments that contributed so much to the final version of this book.

I am most grateful to Tom Curtin and Jeni Ogilvie of Waveland Press for their encouragement and their suggestions. Any author is lucky to have Jeni as an editor. I extend my deepest thanks to Tom, Jeni, and Waveland Press for their commitment to presenting anthropological research to undergraduate students in an interesting and accessible format, making an invaluable contribution to the discipline of cultural anthropology.

Chapter One

Cultural Diversity in a Changing World

Passionate love is a dangerous thing, or so many cultures, folk tales, and stories say. Romantic love can and often does disrupt social relations—it is a turbulent and complex human emotion. Many tales provide warnings about . . . how to avoid being misled, manipulated, seduced . . . by an attractive or ill-meaning lover.

— William Jankowiak (2018)

In the ideology of most people who grew up in the United States, sexual desire, **romantic love**, and **marriage** are intimately interrelated, but this is not true in all societies. As anthropologist William Jankowiak and Edward Fischer (1992) note, and as described in this book, romantic love, a strong sexual and emotional attachment between individuals, appears to be universal, but in many societies it has nothing to do with the choice of a spouse; the needs of the kinship group and the family dominate in choosing a mate. In these cultures romantic love between individuals is often considered dangerous and is repressed in the interests of the larger society. As each of the book's chapters indicates, the idea of romantic love as the basis of marriage is new and challenging in many cultures around the world.

IS MARRIAGE UNIVERSAL? THE NA OF CHINA

While some form of marriage exists in almost all societies, there are a few societies, like the Na (also called the Mosuo) of Southwest

China, where there is no marriage or even a word for it. Among the Na, men and women are joined in a sexual and reproductive partnership in which a man secretly passes a night in his lover's household and returns to his own family in the morning. As lovers, their relationship involves affection, respect, and intimacy but does not include notions of fidelity, permanence, or paternal responsibility for children. Both women and men have multiple partners, serially or simultaneously, and no records are kept of visits to ascertain the paternity of children. There are no Na words for incest, illegitimate child, infidelity, or promiscuity. The lineage is traced through women, and children by different fathers stay in their mother's house for their entire lives. The Na male's "visit," called a *walking marriage*, has been part of their culture for more than a thousand years (Hua 2001; Mattison, Scelza, and Blumenfield 2014; Mattison et al. 2015; Qin 2015).

CULTURAL DIVERSITY AND CHANGE

The Na walking marriage is a rare example, but it illustrates the wide human cultural diversity regarding sexuality, marriage, and family. Other cultural patterns exist that are also very different from those in the West. The view that marriage is, or should be, based on romantic love is generally viewed as a "modern" institution that emerged in Britain and North America around the seventeenth century (Coontz 2005). In the contemporary world, the relationship between sexuality, love, marriage, and family is changing, even in remote traditional societies (Goleman 1992). Affectionate love, the love people have for their parents, their children, and their friends, appears universal (Dettwyler 2011:87), but romantic love is not a part of all cultural systems, although it is widespread in mythology and folklore. Anthropologists in the twentieth century largely focused on the role of kinship in marriages, but today anthropologists are looking more deeply at the role of romantic love in different cultures (Jankowiak 2018; Jankowiak and Paladino 2008). While some current research suggests that romantic love has always been more widespread than previously believed, romantic love as the basis for marriage is largely due to the spread of Western, particularly North American, culture in the late twentieth and early twenty-first centuries. Through social media, films, television, and the internet, sexuality, love, and personal intimacy are now playing a greater role in marriage throughout the world.

In spite of this trend, the emerging relationships between sexuality, romantic love, marriage, and family are still very different in every society, as illustrated in this text. These differences depend on local economic, cultural, political, social, legal, and religious contexts. This diversity has become a "hot" topic as illustrated by the six-week CNN television program, *Sex and Love around the World*, which aired in March 2018. Some twentieth-century social science research emphasized the spread of Westernization as a uniform process of change, driving all cultures in the same direction. A closer look, however, indicates that the spread of new cultural patterns takes different paths in various societies and happens at different speeds.

An important question related to cultural diversity is whether sexuality, romantic love, marriage, and family ties are biologically based on a universal human need for intimacy and reproduction (Fisher 2016) or whether these are culturally created adaptations in response to local conditions. Twentieth-century cultural and social anthropologists emphasized kinship and family ties, rather than romantic love between a married couple, as the basic social bond in human societies. With regard to the universality of romantic love, anthropologists Lynn M. Thomas and Jennifer Cole ask, "Is [romantic] love a universal emotion intrinsic to the human soul . . . or is it produced through specific historical processes and cultural formations?" (2009:2). Answers to these questions reflect a general agreement in the social sciences that human biology, evolution, and culture all play important roles in explaining the universality of romantic love, though not necessarily as the basis for marriage (Brettell and Sargent 2017; Hirsch et al 2009; Hirsch and Wardlow 2006).

The aim of this book is to illustrate the many different ways in which romantic love and companionate marriage (see the discussion below) are finding a place in diverse cultures around the world.

UNDERSTANDING CULTURE

Culture plays an essential role in how humans have adapted to different environments. One useful definition of culture refers to the learned practices, ideas, and symbols shared by a group of people that guide their behavior as members of a particular society. Most people in all societies consider their own culture as natural and right and usually take it for granted. This tendency for people to think that their culture is the best way, or the only way, is called **ethnocentrism**. Cultural anthropology primarily examines culture from the point of view of people in the society being described, in order to gain a deeper understanding of a culture and reduce ethnocentrism by outsiders. This is particularly important in our increasingly globalized world where more people from diverse cultures connect with each other both through direct contact and through global media outlets.

Because sexuality, romantic love, marriage, and family, as well as gender roles, are so deeply embedded in a society, they are particularly difficult for outsiders to understand and for insiders to look at objectively. Globalization is not new: due to exploration, wars, trade, migration, and other activities, different societies have been in contact for hundreds, even thousands of years. What is perhaps new is the speed with which changes are occurring and the deep impact of contemporary globalization on previously more isolated cultures and societies.

Cultural anthropology focuses on both the culture of a particular society and the contrasts and similarities among cultures of different societies; it is largely based on the practice of **fieldwork**, which involves the anthropologist's long-term immersion in the society he or she studies while participating as much as possible in the lives of ordinary people in that society. Fieldwork also includes more formal methods, such as individual and group interviews, taking videos and photographs, documenting genealogies, collecting statistical data, and creating maps and diagrams, all of which provide data on culture. With the increasing importance of cultural change, anthropologists today usually focus on exploring a few cultural patterns in depth, setting them in the wider cultural context, as is the case in this book.

THE FUNCTIONS OF MARRIAGE AND FAMILY

Because of the many forms of marriage around the world, defining marriage is not easy. Anthropological evidence indicates that in spite of very diverse values and practices related to marriage, some form of marriage and family appears as the most common solution to basic human needs. For example, one universal and basic function of marriage is the regulation of sexual access between males and females. This important function is related to the potentially continuous receptivity of humans to sexual activity. If sexual competition was not regulated and channeled into stable, socially approved relationships, it could cause conflict and even chaos in society.

Marriage is also a satisfactory means of organizing labor, assigning responsibility for children and child care, providing a clear framework for individual rights and obligations, and generating rules for the transfer of property and social status between generations. These societal practices are guided by cultural rules that adapt to economic and other aspects of social life. Marriage can thus be usefully defined as a publically, legally, or ritually recognized union between sexually cohabiting adults, between them and any children they take responsibility for, and between the culturally recognized kin of the married couple. There are some rare exceptions to this definition. Among some

African societies, woman–woman marriage is an alternative to heterosexual marriages. This pattern allows a barren woman to divorce her husband, take another woman as her wife, and arrange for a surrogate to impregnate the woman. This relationship does not involve sexual activity between the two women. Children born from this arrangement become members of the barren woman's lineage and refer to her as their father (Kilbride 2006).

Marriage laws are generated by every contemporary national government, although in some West African nations, civil law's controls of marriage are weak, and marriages take place without the sanction of civil law (Whitehouse 2018). Laws governing marriage refer to the legal requirements that determine the validity of a marriage, usually confirmed by a marriage ceremony, called a wedding, and performed by a recognized civil or religious leader. These laws shape the rights and obligations between marriage partners, a married couple and their children, and frequently between the kin of the bride and groom. Marriage is shaped not only by formal law but also by cultural and social factors such as gender roles, economics, courtship, mate selection, family and kinship structures, ideas about chastity and fidelity, symbols, rituals surrounding marriage, marriage preferences and prohibitions. The almost universal rules for marital separation suggest that marital relationships may be relatively stable, but are not necessarily permanent.

MARRIAGE AND KINSHIP

National marriage laws often involve restrictions such as age limits, the sex of the spouses, or the number of spouses permitted. Marriage laws are open to change, primarily due to changing government ideologies regarding individual autonomy and civil rights. In China, for example, concepts of love and marriage practices changed markedly as the country moved from an imperial government to Communism. In imperial times marriages were largely arranged, but under Communism individuals were encouraged to choose their own mates. All societies also specify from which groups a marriage partner is allowed to be chosen (**endogamy**) and which groups are excluded for marital choice (**exogamy**). Societies also specify the permitted number of spouses, for example, one spouse (**monogamy**), or more than one spouse (**polygamy**). Polygamy is divided into two categories: more than one wife (**polygyny**) and more than one husband (**polyandry**).

Family and **kinship systems** that trace ties through males are called **patrilineal**; where these ties are traced through females, societies are defined as matrilineal. Patrilineal societies are usually patrilocal: the married couple lives with the husband's family. Matrilineal societies are usually **matrilocal**: the married couple lives with the wife's family. In **bilateral** kinship systems, like the United States, where kinship is traced through both male and the female lines, the married couple ideally lives independently (**neolocal**), in a nuclear family. These different types of families have both benefits and problems, particularly for the spouse who is viewed, at least initially, as the family outsider, as illustrated in the chapters on India and China.

Rules prohibiting sexual relations between certain relatives are known as **incest taboos**, which are universal, though defined differently in different societies. Unlike the United States, for example, where first cousins are prohibited from marrying in most states, some societies prefer marriage between certain kinds of cousins, indicating that incest taboos are culturally, not necessarily biologically, mandated. Some social scientists explain the apparently universal taboo on parents engaging in sex with their children, or siblings having sex with each other, to a revulsion toward sexual relations between close kin who have grown up together. Other social scientists argue that forcing people to marry outside their kin group extends the social alliances necessary for group survival. When the anthropologist Margaret Mead asked a man in New Guinea if he was allowed to marry his sister, he was astonished. "If a man married his sister" he replied, "he would have no brother-in-law with whom to hunt, to garden, or to visit" (in Lévi-Strauss 1969/1949:485).

As illustrated in this text, in some societies, marriage is very often arranged by parents of the bride and groom, while in others, like the United States, the bride and groom make the choice. Individual choice is a cultural pattern that is gaining acceptance in a wide range of societies. Even where individual choice of spouses is valued, however, parental influence on marital choice, regarding, for example, class, race, ethnicity, and other factors, almost always plays a role. Most societies have formal and/or informal rules, about the exchange of goods, gifts, cash, or services that must accompany a marriage. Bridewealth is the term most often used for transfers from the groom's family to the bride's family, and dowry is used for the transfer of goods by the bride's family to the groom's family.

COMPANIONATE MARRIAGE

One of the most significant changes identified with the modern world that emerged in Britain and North America around the seventeenth century is the importance of romantic love as a basis for marriage and the ideal of **companionate marriage** (Hirsch and Wardlow

2006). Companionate marriage puts a greater emphasis on sexuality as a source of pleasure between the spouses, rather than being only for reproductive purposes and tends to be linked with individual choice of mates. The term also implies that each spouse expects to be the other's "best friend" spending more time with each other than with family members or same-sex friends. Companionate marriage reflects a change from the social pattern in families based on gender role segregation, with the husband providing economic support and the wife providing domestic and reproductive labor. With more women working outside the home, there is now a trend toward husbands and wives sharing economic, household, and child-rearing duties.

Although companionate marriages existed in some ancient cultures and small-scale societies, it is generally viewed as a "modern" institution. Companionate marriage contrasts with the socioeconomic- or politically-based marriage alliances formerly controlled by kin groups, once found in most cultures around the world. Capitalism, industrialization, and the greater emphasis on individual freedom due to the spread of Protestant religions are basic to the development of companionate marriage.

Throughout the world, increasing globalization, changing governmental policies, new economies, and new technologies are challenging traditional marriage arrangements and family structures. Extended families, which contain three or more generations, and large households are mainly adapted to agrarian and herding societies, and nuclear families to both hunting and gathering societies and modern industrial societies. Now, with population increase, the spread of global capitalism, urbanization, and expanding employment in industry, information technology, and the service sectors of the economy, traditional family structures and the selection of marriage partners, together with their associated gender roles, have significantly changed. Fueling that change is the continual development of new technologies of social connection such as the internet, cell phones, and social media, which facilitates the opportunity to seek romantic relationships. The internet dating industry is a worldwide multibillion-dollar business. It is widely used by people living within the same society as well as by people seeking mates from societies other than their own, for both romantic and economic reasons (Nakamatsu 2011).

GENDER ROLES

Sex refers to the biological distinctions between males and females. **Gender** refers to the cultural patterns associated with sex differences. Every society defines **gender roles**, or behavior appropriate to men and women, as central to cultural patterns of sexuality, marriage, and family. In a patriarchy or male-dominated society, men have greater power, status, and control compared to women. Most of the world's societies are patriarchal; whether there are or ever have been any matriarchal societies is subject to debate, as noted in chapter 7's discussion of the Minangkabau of Indonesia. But in almost all societies, even where men and women are theoretically considered equal, the roles individuals play, in the family, in public, in the economic, political, and religious systems, and in sexual and love relations, are almost always determined by gender. The diverse relationship between gender roles, culture and sexuality, marriage, and family patterns is illustrated in the different societies described in the chapters in this book.

Globalization significantly affects changes in gender roles, particularly the power relationships between men and women. These changes are also affecting cultural patterns regarding sexuality, marriage, and family. One major global change is the increase in the number of women entering the workforce outside the home, as described in the chapters on Iran, Indonesia, and China. People in many cultures now marry much later than previously, if they marry at all. In Japan, Taiwan, South Korea, and Hong Kong, the average age for marriage is now 29–30 years for women and 31–33 for men, while in 1970 the averages were 23.6 and 27.3 respectively (Jones 2010; Lau 2017). In 2010, a third of Japanese women entering their 30s were unmarried, and many of these women will never marry (*Economist* 2011). By 2015, the percentage of people in Asia 30–34 years of age who were unmarried was 47 percent for men and 35 percent for women. Between the ages of 25 and 35 years, 60 percent of men and 50 percent of women were not married (Yamada 2017).

FAMILY STRUCTURES

Reproduction is also decreasing around the world. In agricultural or herding societies, children are a good economic investment; the cost of raising children is relatively low and they contribute in to the family economy by caring for animals, tending gardens, and performing other duties. But in urban societies, it costs more to raise children and pay for their education, and the economic benefits to their families thus shrink. It is not clear how today's trends will affect family structures in the future; in monogamous societies, if the economic values of marriage and children continue to decline, will two-parent families disappear? No one knows the answer. Humans are adaptable creatures, and we have the ability to create new cultural forms as we have done in the past in order to survive and thrive in a changing world.

BOOK OUTLINE

As indicated above, the central theme of this book is the diverse ways in which romantic love and companionate marriage are being incorporated into a wide range of societies in the context of global and local changes. Each society is unique, and the chapter titles reflect a central feature of the society related to these changes. The questions at the end of each chapter stimulate reflection on the cultural themes and adaptations to change explored in that chapter.

Chapter 2 discusses some ideal and actual cultural patterns of sexuality, love, marriage, gender, and family in the United States, some ways in which these are contested, and some of the changes occurring in the present time.

Chapter 3 describes the changes regarding sex, love, marriage, and family that have taken place in China, as the country moved from an imperial past to a Communist present. As the chapter demonstrates, despite significant changes regarding love, marriage, and family, some traditional patterns remain and become integrated with contemporary practices such as free choice in marriage, romantic love, and wide, though restricted, use of the internet.

Chapter 4 describes love marriages and arranged marriages in India, which are both similar to and different from China. India, like China, illustrates how the modern ideology of love, free choice of spouses, and the increasing opportunities for women to become educated and to work outside the home contest, but at the same time adapt to, traditional forms of arranged marriage, rather than strictly replacing them.

Chapter 5, which focuses on Brazilian shantytowns, describes how extreme poverty affects ideas and practices regarding sexuality, love, and marriage, and the difficulties of incorporating ideologies of romance and companionate marriage into an economic system that deprives men of the stable income needed to support a family.

Chapter 6 sets the current underground sexual revolution in the Islamic Republic of Iran in the context of the broader philosophy and morality of Islam, regarding sexuality, love, marriage, and female modesty.

Chapter 7, like chapter 6, examines the impact of Islam in the Muslim nation of Indonesia, as it affects sexuality, love, marriage and the family among a traditional matrilineal ethnic group, the Minangkabau. This chapter explores the issue of matriarchal power, which strongly contrasts with power established by traditional Islamic doctrine.

Chapter 8, describing the Igbo of Nigeria, also illustrates the impact of religion on culture. The Igbo avidly embrace the doctrine of love as the basis for marriage, significantly due to both the influence of Christian missionaries and the spread of a global economy. The chapter also demonstrates that romantic love and companionate marriage exist side by side with gender inequality and widespread male infidelity, leading to the spread of HIV.

Chapter 9, on the South Pacific, notes the important role of Christian missionaries, along with the impact of US colonialism, in shaping traditional societies. The chapter examines both the facts and fantasies associated with South Pacific sexuality illuminated by the fieldwork of the widely known anthropologist Margaret Mead.

In Chapter 10, the rare pattern of fraternal polyandry, or multiple husbands, is described for Himalayan ethnic groups. The description shows how polyandry is shaped both by the Buddhist religion and by the difficult mountain economy. Once in decline, polyandry, along with romantic love, appears to be having a revival under the impact of current economic and cultural changes.

Chapter 11 traces the diversity of LGBTQ people and their lives, both historically and culturally, from ancient Greece to modern Indonesia. It highlights the global realm of same-sex marriage.

Chapter 12 summarizes key topics and cultural similarities and differences discussed in the previous chapters.

This book aims to offer a better understanding of the changing patterns of sexuality, love, marriage, gender, and family, both within and among diverse societies throughout the world. The description and analysis of the various cultures help further a major task of social science: to see each of the world's cultures not in terms of superiority or inferiority, but rather as one of many possible adaptations to specific environments in an increasingly globalized world.

Chapter Two

Contradictions, Conflicts, and Change
The United States

In the United States, partly thanks to Sigmund Freud, sexual desire is seen as a universal and natural instinct, rooted in human biology. Cultural anthropology argues that sexuality is also powerfully shaped by culture and that it is perhaps impossible to say where "nature" leaves off and "culture" begins.

—Alma Gottlieb (2002)

Cultural anthropology helps us to reimagine the ideas we often take for granted concerning sexuality, love, marriage, and family. In this chapter, we examine the ideologies and practices in the United States regarding these concepts and examine how they have changed over time.

SEXUALITY

In China, romance has a lot to do with politics and not so much to do with sex, while in the United States romance has nothing to do with politics and everything to do with sex.

— Chinese student

The young student quoted above (see chapter 3) enviously contrasts the control that the authoritarian Chinese government exerts over love relationships with the individualism and freedom allowed in the United States. All over the world, people admire the enjoyment of free sex, romantic love, and marriage as they think it exists in the United States. Outsiders' views of this ideology are largely based on US popular culture portrayed in films, on television, on the internet, and in print media, which has traveled around the world and significantly influenced other societies. An important question explored in this chapter is, how realistic are these portrayals and understandings?

Patriarchy became dominant throughout the world, including in the United States, with the emergence of, first, agricultural economies and then industrialization. Patriarchal societies significantly expanded their control over sexual behavior, particularly regarding women; men were granted more sexual freedom, more sexual power, and greater license to transgress sexual norms, even with regard to being violent, without being held responsible. But, as the #MeToo movement indicates, this is changing, slowly but surely. The movement was established in 2006 to find solutions to sexual violence and help survivors of it. It has spawned a national dialogue about sexual violence and emboldened women to tell their stories.

Changes regarding male sexual dominance have occurred for many reasons; perhaps a major one is a huge increase in the number of women employed outside the home. Another factor is the availability of artificial methods of birth control that led to major shifts in sexual behavior. The birth control pill and IUD devices, introduced in the 1960s, gave women more power and control. It is hard to believe, but it was only in the early 1970s that contraception was made legal for married couples in the United States, abortion was legalized under certain conditions, and nonheterosexual orientation was no longer officially considered a mental disorder. In the mid-twentieth century, the publication of the Kinsey Reports on sexual behavior in human males and females had an enormous impact on normalizing sexual desire. Beginning in the 1960s, the sexual revolution, the rise of feminism, and the LGBT (now LGBTQ) movement also made sexuality less stigmatized. Acceptance of sexual intercourse outside of marriage increased, aided now by more easily available methods of birth control (Bowman 2018).

Religious moral codes are central in most societies, including the United States, in guiding sexual ideology and behavior. Christian religions generally hold that sexual relations are a sacred act between a man and a woman and should only be performed within marriage; Catholicism, for example, holds that sex is for the purpose of procreation. Christianity also characterizes certain sexual practices, such as anal or oral copulation (sodomy), as shameful or sinful, emphasizes control over one's sexual drives, and supports virginity before marriage. Many religious communities, such as evangelical, strongly oppose abortion. Christian missionaries have been active for centuries in spreading these doctrines around the world.

Public discussion about sexuality, self-help books, media representations of sexuality, and sex education have expanded since the mid-twentieth century, contributing to the vision, both within the United States and of outsiders, that the United States is the "land of the free" when it comes to sexuality. In fact, however, surveys indicate that US attitudes regarding sexuality are substantially more restrictive than that of other industrialized societies. One international survey indicates that 30 percent of people in the United States consider premarital sex as always wrong, compared to an average of 10% percent in six other Western nations. Similar differences were found regarding the condemnation of sex before the age of 16, extramarital sex, and same-gender sexual behavior. Some of these restrictive attitudes particularly apply to women, because it is widely believed that men have more sexual urges than women, which results in a "double standard." For example, it is more strongly disapproved for women to engage in premarital sex unless they are "in love" than it is for men (Dettwyler 2011:105–111).

Restrictions on sex education in the United States reflect prudishness, compared, for example, with the industrialized nations of Europe; perhaps correlated with these restrictions, the US also has the highest teen-aged pregnancy rate in the industrialized world. The contrasts between attitudes in the United States and Europe are evident in ads for condoms: a German ad says, "Give the gift of love," and a US ad says, "If you're going to have sex, don't get screwed." Since popular media is the main public source of knowledge about sex for adolescents in the United States, perhaps a more positive yet still protective ideology should replace the fear-based and abstinence-based approaches in both popular media and sex education designed for American teenagers (European Sex Attitudes . . . 2010).

Sexuality and beauty—female physical attractiveness—are linked. This link is expressed in both ancient and contemporary mythology in the United States and around the world. Here, it is fostered by Hollywood films, television advertising, popular magazines, and internet dating. The beauty and fashion industries have become billion-dollar consumer enterprises, which thrive both in socialist as well as capitalist societies, and in both cases, a woman's physical beauty is an important characteristic in attracting a spouse.

Ideals regarding women's beauty are culturally patterned, diverse, and changing. The importance of these ideals is exemplified by the sometimes extreme efforts girls and women make to attain an attractive appearance. Many who have grown up in the United States might be repelled by how beauty was and is shaped in other societies, without realizing the parallels to their own culture. In the nineteenth century, Europeans and North Americans cringed at the "barbaric" Chinese practice of foot binding, but today seem largely unconscious of the great pain and often permanent disfigurement suffered by Western women who wear the high heeled shoes valued by contemporary fashion (Lenkeit 2019). The rings around the necks of Thai tribal women, the surgical transformation of Asian eyes, and the fattening of marriageable women in Africa may seem bizarre to us, but objectively they are no more bizarre than the widespread anorexia caused by American women imitating fashion models; "nose jobs"; surgical face-lifts, Botox treatments, and breast enlargements; and torture at the dentist's office in search of more beautiful teeth (Miner 2016/1956). US women seem to be equally willing to endure pain to heighten their sexual attraction, just as women are in other cultures.

LOVE AND MARRIAGE

People around the world are of the opinion that in the United States a happy marriage is based on the emotional ties of romantic love and affection, intimacy, and pleasure. With globalization, this ideal of **companionate marriage** has diffused throughout the world, though in different ways and with different results. And even in the United States, it is one thing to marry for love and another to stay married for love. The high divorce rate (approximately 50 percent) and domestic/intimate partner violence (24 people per minute; Breiding, Chen, and Black 2014) in the United States challenges this idealized view of marriage, leading many couples in this country to seek alternatives to marriage.

These statistics make it easy to see that the emotional bond found in companionate marriage and its feature of romantic love, which privileges the married couple over all other family ties, comes with many risks. Companionate marriage stresses the importance of individual fulfillment and also the ideal of individuality—stating our love for a particular person means we think that person would be a more satisfying and pleasurable partner than any other because of his or her specific characteristics. This ideal, however, may not provide a stable future for marital happiness.

The North American view of love and its relationship to commitment is most explicitly and extensively defined by anthropologist Helen Fisher, who is the chief scientific advisor to the dating site Match.com. Fisher conducts an annual survey of single people in the United States to find out their views on who they love, why they love, and how the answers to these questions relate to the importance of love in their interpersonal relationships. Unlike in North America's preindustrial past, today, according to Fisher's surveys, financial security plays only a small role in marriage; 86 percent of the singles she inter-

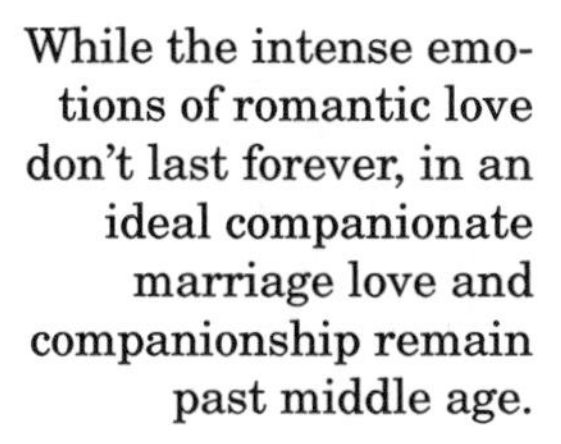
While the intense emotions of romantic love don't last forever, in an ideal companionate marriage love and companionship remain past middle age.

viewed seek a "committed partner" to share their lives; over 90 percent want someone who respects them, who they can trust and confide in, who makes them laugh, and who makes enough time for them—a person first and foremost whom they define as a "soul mate." More than half her survey population believe in love at first sight, and almost 90 percent believe you can stay married to the same person forever. Even many survey respondents who say they don't want to marry give as their reason that "you don't need to marry to prove that you love someone"; a third of the respondents agreed it was acceptable to leave a satisfactory marriage if you are no longer in love (Fisher 2016:300).

In the United States, while romantic love is still viewed as the most important basis for marriage, marriage is no longer viewed as the necessary outcome of love, and has become optional (Fisher 2016). The methods of meeting people suitable for dating has also changed; for example, there are fewer "blind dates." In the past, I fixed up lots of my friends and was thrilled when many of them got married. Those days are pretty much over. Now the internet is widely used for meeting and dating people; many singles who are age 30 and above and looking for a long-term relationship use the dating site eharmony.com. Adolescents use internet sites for fun: companionship, someone to talk to, and developing casual relationships. Tinder is an example of a site geared to fun and "hookups." Research indicates that many relationships formed on the internet primarily involve passion and excitement but do not include commitment and other kinds of support that are important for marital happiness (Haack and Falcke 2014).

In these changing times, one alternative to a committed relationship is "hooking up," a "no-strings-attached," uncommitted sexual encounter between two people not in a romantic relationship. Well over half the singles in Helen Fisher's research reported having engaged in a "one-night stand"—more men (60 percent) than women (50 percent). College students admitted it was most often because they were attracted to a person and wanted to show their affection. Many of the singles also stated they hoped "hooking up" would lead to a traditional romantic relationship, so perhaps Fisher is correct in regarding the increasing number of these relationships as "commitment-lite" or "slow love" (Fisher 2016:308–309).

While companionate marriage emphasizes sexual pleasure between a married couple, North Americans have long expressed skepticism that intense sexual desire is a good basis for a happy, stable marriage. This is illustrated in Tennessee Williams' 1947 play, *A Streetcar Named Desire*, where Blanche warns her sister against marrying the passionate object of her desire, Stanley Kowalski: "A man like that is someone to go out with once—twice, three times when the devil is in you. But live with? Have a child by?" This contrast between erotic adventure and excitement versus the stability of domesticity is perhaps related to the high US rate of marital infidelity and divorce, but it also appears to be universal. Nisa, a !Kung woman of the Kalahari Desert in Africa, distinguishes between the stable affection she feels for her husband and the passionate and exciting, though fleeting, feeling she has for her lovers: "When two people come together their hearts are on fire and their passion is very great. After a while, the fire cools and that's how it stays" (Shostak 1981:266–269).

Nisa was an older woman in a longtime marriage, so North Americans might be surprised at the revelation about her affairs. In the United States, love and sexual activity are mainly identified in the media as a monopoly of the young. The presentation of sexuality and beauty in advertisements as a lure for consumers mainly features young models. While in many societies, in Asia, for example, it is considered shameful to think of older and even middle-aged women as interested in sex, in the United States, love and even sex among older people is increasing, although in one anthropological study of older women in the United States, using in-depth interviews, only a few even wanted to talk about the role of sexuality as they aged (Joans 2013). Attitudes toward marriage among the elderly vary by sex: elderly widowed or divorced males are twice as interested in dating and remarriage as elderly women (Klinenberg 2012). It may be that elderly women don't want to take on the care of an aging man who is likely to die before them, and elderly men have more options as there are fewer of them (Dettwyler personal communication 2018).

THE CHANGING FAMILY

I hear that in America if you want to visit your parents you have to make an appointment with them.

This statement was directed to me by an older woman living with her son's family when I was doing **fieldwork** in Mumbai, India. I was a little taken aback by what she obviously meant as a criticism, but then I realized she was right: my parents were very active and I could never count on them being home so I needed to call them before I came to visit. US culture still generally favors the independent, **heterosexual**, **nuclear family**—husband, wife and children—living together on their own. Today, however, many families, often by necessity rather than preference, deviate from this ideal. This is partly caused by a high divorce rate, and the growing number of working mothers and single-parent households, unmarried couples living together in long-term relationships, childless couples, people who never marry and remain in their parents' home, others who remarry after divorce or widowhood, and of three-generation households (Parenting in America 2015).

The high rates of divorce and remarriage also enmesh nuclear families in larger and more complicated kinship networks. Sometimes called "blended families," these networks include previously divorced spouses and their new partners, children from previous marriages, and multiple sets of grandparents or other kin. Blended families may function in some ways like traditional two-parent families but, in fact, only one child in six averages a weekly visit with a divorced father, and only one in four sees him once a month. Almost half the children of divorced parents have not seen their biological father for more than a year, and more than two-thirds have lost contact with him ten years later (Hacker 2012).

Another change in the US is the growing number of multigenerational families, which has increased substantially since 1970. This increase is partly due to the larger number of recent immigrants who live in such families (Kramer 2011) and also to an increase in the number of adult children moving back to their parental home because they cannot find employment. At the same time, the number of people living alone is also rising, including young people, middle-aged people, and the elderly (Klinenberg 2012).

In 2009, single-parent households in the United States, mainly single-mother households, accounted for about 27 percent of all households with children, and 3.1 million American children lived with neither of their parents (they lived with foster parents or grandparents) (Kreider and Ellis 2011). One study estimates that about half the children in the United States will spend at least some of their childhood in a single-parent family, either as the result of divorce or separation or because their mother never married (Luker 1996).

The number of children born to unmarried mothers is an important and increasing trend in the United States, reaching over 40 percent across all maternal ages and over 50 percent for children born to women under the age of 30. In the past, unmarried mothers were mainly teenagers; today, most unmarried mothers are between ages 20 and 30. Although birth rates of unmarried mothers are up for all ethnic groups in the United States (36.9 percent in 2005 and 39.8 percent in 2016; National Center for Health Statistics 2018), among Hispanic women the figure is 53 percent of all births and among African American women it reaches 73 percent of all births (Wildsmith, Steward-Streng and Manlove 2011; Banks 2011). As a group, single-mother families are far poorer than other families (DeParle 2012). One exception to the trend of single motherhood is college graduates, for whom marriage makes more sense economically than it does for poor women whose mates are less likely to have well-paying jobs, or even to be employed (Cherlin 2014; Miller and Alderman 2014; Dettwyler 2011).

At the same time, many young adults are having fewer children, and many others are not sure they ever want to have children. In 2018, the fertility rate in the United States was at a record low for the second year in a row; it is now almost equal to the lower fertility rates in the rest of the industrialized world. Prior to this time, the US had higher fertility rates than most Western countries due to more teenage pregnancies, more unintended pregnancies, and high fertility rates among Hispanic immigrants. These trends have reversed, partly because of the increased use of birth control methods like IUDs. The declining fertility rate is mainly due to issues of economic insecurity and gender equality. As more women are working, their desire to have children is decreasing or being delayed. Wanting more freedom and more leisure time, and the current expenses of child care, also help explain the decline in fertility (Miller 2018).

Another change in American families is the care of the elderly. Aging is a universal biological aspect of being human but must be understood within a cultural context (Sokolofsky 2009). One essential question every society must address is "who will care for the aged?" In many cultures today, particularly outside the West, the family is considered the natural place for its older members, although this is changing: even in traditional societies like India and China, institutional residential care for the elderly is expanding. But the question of who will care for the aged is particularly poignant in the United States: with the advent of modern medicine, old age is frequently associated with a long dying process and incapacitating diseases; as a result, many forms of institutionalized care such as assisted living facilities, nursing homes, and memory care facilities are now in place, although family support is still considered essential.

Caring for elderly family members can impose many burdens, especially if the elderly person is widowed or in poor health, if family finances are tight, if all the children are working professionals, as is increasingly the case, or if a group's religion and cultural beliefs emphasize caring for one's parents in the home, as is the case with

Islam. Many US Muslims are struggling with their ability to provide care for their aging parents, but putting elderly parents in nursing homes is unthinkable. The Qur'an admonishes that children care for their elderly relatives at home, and, indeed, options for culturally appropriate care outside the home do not exist (Alfarah et al. 2012). One new idea is to adjoin nursing homes to mosques, providing communal prayer rooms; serving halal food; providing same-sex medical and nursing care; and adding multilingual staff (Clemetson 2006). Nevertheless, skirting religious beliefs and strongly held cultural beliefs to provide institutionalized care for elders does not seem possible in the foreseeable future.

Another US group shouldering the responsibility of elder care is women. In a study conducted by Angelina Grigoryeva (2017) daughters provide an average of 12.3 hours of elderly parent care per month as compared to sons' 5.6 hours, despite constraints, such as employment or childcare.

As in other aspects of family structure, economics, culture, public policy, and personal family factors all play a role in who cares for the elderly. This is just one area where changes are taking place as part of the attempts to accommodate political, social, and particularly economic changes in our globalizing world. Other changes are also occurring regarding, for example, increasing interclass, interethnic, and same-sex marriage. These new relationships bring benefits but may also be a source of tension and even trauma within families. All changes require time to fit into a culture, but as Helen Fisher puts it, change is here to stay. Optimistically, changes regarding sex, love, marriage, gender roles, and family will benefit society and also result in more individual satisfaction regarding our closest and most intimate relationships.

1. Describe three important US cultural patterns regarding sexuality, romantic love, and marriage.
2. Which of the many changes in the United States described in this chapter do you think are most beneficial and which least beneficial to the larger society. Explain your reasons.
3. Describe some important changes regarding how gender is implicated in sexuality, romantic love, marriage and family in the United States. Why do you think these changes have occurred?
4. Explain the role that beauty plays in sex, love, and marriage in US society.

Chapter Three

From Past to Present
Love and Marriage in China

A virtuous woman will enter the household
Sons will multiply and prosperity increase.

— Frank Ching (2009)

MARRIAGE IN IMPERIAL CHINA

In China's long history, marriage, family, and intimate emotional relations between men and women were primarily shaped by the imperial culture (2100 B.C.E. to 1912 C.E.) and Confucian philosophy (whose influence began in sixth century B.C.E. and continued on and off into the thirteenth century C.E.). Confucian ideology existed, with varying levels of emphasis, throughout the duration of imperial China. China's economy was based on plow agriculture, which supported a large, rapidly growing population, the rise of great cities, and a centralized government bureaucracy, presided over by the emperor. Elite scholar-intellectuals, state officials, and large landowners dominated the lower classes of peasants, merchants, artisans, and domestic laborers. Despite many changes that have occurred since 1912, traditional cultural values and practices have continued, though the integration of the past and the present is not without anxiety, contradictions, and conflict.

The ideal family was built on patriarchy, patriliny, patrilocality, filial piety, and the interests of the collective, which eclipsed those of the individual. Ancestor worship was a central ritual, and all homes contained an ancestral shrine honoring mainly male, ancestors. At the shrine, descendants expressed their religious obligation to continue the male line and the importance of having sons. Marriage was arranged by elders with no role for individual choice. Passion and love occasionally played a role in some marital relationships in the late imperial era, but this was a clear breach of the dominant cultural values (Ebrey 1990). Spouses never met until their wedding day; an arranged marriage, with a wife who was a stranger to her husband, was less likely to undermine a married son's obedience and loyalty to his parents, particularly his father, and their control over the household (Stockard 2002:45).

At marriage, a woman moved into her husband's parents' home; men dominated women both in the household, which was segregated by sex, and in political and public life. A wife was required to serve and demonstrate respect to her husband and his family and produce male heirs, while a husband's role was to provide for his family. Elite marriages involved elaborate rituals and grand displays of cash and material goods, such as household furnishings and jewelry given to the bride by the groom's family (Chan 2006); the pattern was similar but less elaborate for poorer families. Though ideally families sought marriage partners for their children of approximately equal status, the **extended family** established by marriage was an opportunity to create political and economic alliances used to raise one's social status.

The central importance of elite marriages in imperial China was symbolized by elaborate rituals and displays of material goods, including the lavish parades in which the bride was taken to the groom's household.

Throughout the late imperial era, children generally married in early adolescence. Families in the same lineage, who shared a common last name, were forbidden to marry by both law and custom. Parents engaged a local matchmaker to check the lineage and horoscopes of possible candidates in nearby villages. A family's good standing in the community was important, and any doubts about a girl's virginity excluded her from consideration. The amount of cash (**bridewealth**) paid by the husband's family and the **dowry** of material goods given by the wife's family was fixed before the wedding ceremony. If the dowry did not meet the agreed upon amount, a wife would be badly treated or even sent back to her family. The dowry placed a heavy burden on a bride's family, who knew from her birth that a daughter would not live with them permanently; this is illustrated in the Chinese proverb: "Raising a daughter is like watering another man's garden."

Sons, in contrast to daughters, never left their family home and eventually were responsible for the care of their aged parents. A wife lived her adult life in a house full of strangers at first, and her visits to her own parents were strictly controlled. The mother-in-law exercised supreme authority in the household, and daughters-in-law, who were from different villages, were often in conflict with each other. A wife who created a close bond with her husband strengthened her place in his family, but any public demonstration of marital compatibility threatened the traditional family hierarchy. A wife's best chance to improve her position was to bear sons with whom she established a close and loyal relationship. A man whose wife did not bear sons might take one or more additional wives, which added to family tensions.

CULTURAL CHANGE UNDER COMMUNISM

With the decline of the imperial culture in 1912 and after years of political turmoil and civil wars, in 1949 the successful Communist revolution led by Mao Zedong resulted in the creation of the People's Republic of China. This led to dramatic cultural changes. By 1950, the passage of the New Marriage Law promoted "liberation," specifically mandating free marital choice and gender equality. In 1966, Mao organized the Cultural Revolution in order to further promote Communist ideals, which had not been enthusiastically embraced in all segments of Chinese society. The entrepreneurial, urban, educated middle class had continued to maintain a capitalist individualist orientation stressing professional success, higher education, and social mobility, rather than the well-being of the community. Millions of young people from these families, designated as "class enemies," were forced to drop out of college and relocate to work in rural areas and be "reeducated" by the peasants in order to identify more closely with Communist ideals.

Like other state efforts, the Cultural Revolution only partly succeeded. United States President Richard Nixon's visit to China in 1972 opened an important door to Western, and especially US, culture, which already appealed to Chinese urban youth, especially those who had been sent to the countryside. After Mao's death in 1976, these young adults looked forward to returning to college, rejoining their urban families, seeking higher professional opportunities, and even going abroad. "Going to America is my dream," as one young woman said.

The Communist government's support of free marital choice was driven more by its desire to break from its feudal past, abolish patriarchal traditions, and become a progressive nation than it was by its views of romantic attachment. Personal liaisons between marriageable men and women were still subject to many political restrictions as well as family pressures. Local government officials judged people on their political "reliability," and economic, educational, and social opportunities depended on government permission. This significantly affected rural to urban migration, for which residence permits were (and still are) required (Obendiek 2016). Competition for higher education and urban professions was fierce: so many young people strategically presented themselves as good Communists in order to achieve personal goals. As one young student said, "in China, romance has a lot to do with politics and not so much to do with sex, while in the United States romance has nothing to do with politics and everything to do with sex" (Young, personal communication 2017).

POLITICAL COMMITMENT AND DIVERSITY

These strategies are illustrated in the experience of Shu Lee, a university student in a small, nonindustrial city. Shu Lee had a boyfriend she hoped to marry, but initially he was not interested. He wanted to marry a girl from Shanghai so he could get a permit to work and live there. "In Shanghai," he said, "even the ugly girls get married because everyone wants to live in Shanghai, and marriage is almost the only way." But the local government officials refused his permit to move, teach, and marry in Shanghai, so he remained at the local college and decided to marry Shu Lee, who shared his ambitions. Together they joined local Communist youth organizations hoping this would improve their chances to get teaching positions in Shanghai so that they could live "a good, comfortable life" (Young, personal communication, 1981).

Other young people more sincerely believed in Maoist ideals regarding marriage. "Free marital choice" was not based on the US ideal of romantic love but rather on qualities of friendship, trust, and a companionate commitment to Communist ideology. Shao Jhun, a middle-aged woman in a small city, was officially recognized by the state as a *virtuous wife and good mother.* She says:

> If it hadn't been for the Cultural Revolution, I would have gone to university. But after the Revolution I was assigned to teach in elementary school where a Party member introduced me to my future husband. We never did any courting. We registered our marriage a week after we'd met. He was a construction worker, just out of the [army] and had been selected for an assignment in Africa but wanted to get his private life fixed up before he went. Seeing as how he looked really honest, I accepted him although my family was against him because he was poor . . . he was a Party member who'd been the commissar of a youth organization. Any comrade who's good enough to be an organization cadre is politically reliable. We've had a good life, even if I am much more educated than him. When I was offered an opportunity to go to graduate school, he insisted I take it and he took care of our children. We get along well; we've never had a row. We've got a duty to each other; he made so many sacrifices for our family. Our differences, the less said about them, the better. We've always treated each other with the greatest respect. (quoted in Xinxin and Ye 1987)

THE CONTEMPORARY ERA

Shao Jhun's values are part of traditional Chinese culture. Plum Blossom, a middle-aged married woman from rural China, contrasts her marriage with her parents' marriage by saying, "One needs to [remember] that there are different kinds of love . . . I never heard [my father] say 'I love you.' I think he loves my mother, but . . . for his generation, love was primarily a matter of commitment, work, and duty" (Santos 2016). By the 1980s, a different type of love and marriage, embraced by young people, was spurred by changes in the government's move toward globalization.

After Mao's death in 1976, government reform policies led to more open markets, greater industrial development, urbanization, and economic growth. China's ambition to become a modern economic, political, and cultural global power opened the doors to increasing cultural influence from the West through the media, migration, the internet, and industrialization. This produced a highly consumer-oriented culture, greater social inequality, and a growing middle class. Increasingly, values were now shaped by ideas about modernity, individual choice, and emotional commitments, especially in urban areas. While enthusiastically adopted by many youths, the changes occurring in personal relationships, family commitments, and professional development also caused widespread disorientation and anxiety (Donner and Santos 2016; Farrer 2002).

Government-based reforms were propagated through new laws, feminist organizations, and widespread media propaganda in all areas of life. In 1980 and again in 2001, the 1950 Marriage Law was expanded, enforcing **monogamy** and gender equality and establishing a modern legal framework as the basis of marriage. Arranged marriages and money or gift exchanges were forbidden. National family planning laws were enacted, encouraging "late marriage and late childbirth; the legal marital age for men was raised from 20 to 22 years and for women from 18 to 20 years. Lineage **endogamy** (the practice of marrying inside one's group) continued to be restricted, but newlyweds could now become a member of each other's families and women could use their own names after marriage. Women were given the freedom to work and pursue an education without restrictions from their husbands (Obendiek 2016). Husbands and wives were given equal rights to property acquired during a marriage, which now belonged to both of them. Family relationships included the legal duty for spouses to support and assist each other, for parents to provide for their children, and for grown children to care for their aging parents. Women were formally discouraged from being subservient to their husbands or their in-laws. The new marriage laws encouraged more companionate and intimate conjugal relations; divorce was granted only if both husband and wife agreed, and a continuing relationship between divorced parents and their children was mandatory.

MORE CHANGES

In 1979, the government had strongly enforced a one-child policy aimed at controlling population growth, particularly in the cities. This policy, along with expanded access to ultrasound technology and the traditional preference for sons, increased abortions of female fetuses, resulting in a tremendous imbalance of males to females. In 2015, when the Chinese government became concerned about this imbalance, and its aging population, this law changed to allow married couples to have two children. The preference for sons is slowly changing; in today's prosperous urban families, girls are considered as good as, or sometimes even preferable to, boys. Daughters are emotionally closer to their families and more willing and now more financially able to provide support in their parents' old age (Greenhalgh 2007).

Due to increasing foreign influence, particularly that of the United States, sexual norms are also changing. But while premarital sex is becoming more acceptable, and has even become part of a youth culture in megacities like Shanghai (Farrer 2002), men accept this more than women. Change also holds true for premarital cohabitation: marriage preceded by cohabitation was almost nonexistent in the 1950s–1970s. Since the 1980s, however, as either a preparatory stage of marriage or a trial period of family life, it has become a common pathway to marriage. In one study, evidence was found for a socioeconomic gradient of family formation, with marriage preceded by cohabitation more likely for higher educated men and women (Li n.d.). Marriage trends for women and men in rural and urban areas have developed in tandem with marriage policy and other socioeconomic changes.

But while love and personal intimacy are playing a greater role in Chinese marriages, patriliny, patrilocality, the preference for sons and deference to parental wishes continue to be important. Romantic attachment is more accepted today but is not yet institutionalized in the form of the nuclear household. Nevertheless, even marriage based on affective relationships continues to stress long-term individual and collective acts of mutual assistance. This is particularly true in rural areas where the "marriage market" for men is closely tied to higher education. This places a huge economic burden on rural families and causes deep conflicts as young people weigh personal marital choice against their financial obligations to their families (Obendiek 2016). Rural women also still remain largely responsible for domestic work and are expected to put their husbands and families before themselves.

Marriages based on love between two individuals is increasingly important in contemporary China, particularly in urban areas. The role of the family is still important, however, particularly in providing economic support and in the focus on the patrilineal ancestral line.

The government's strong support of capitalism and an extremely consumer-oriented culture are expressed in government-sponsored media, propaganda, and advertisements promoting romance as the "lifeblood of modern marriage," but the contemporary emphasis on social status and income now cause great anxiety within the government and in public opinion. Traditionally, marriage in China was preferred between families of equal social standing, though more for families seeking wives for their sons than husbands for their daughters. Today, however, partly due to the gender imbalance, upward social mobility and a comfortable or even luxurious lifestyle is a central marital goal for many women (Obendiek 2016).

Ambivalence about these new values is widespread. This is indicated by the national publicity and debate generated by a recent episode on the government-sponsored TV dating site, called "If You Are the One." A young male participant invited a female participant, Ma Nuo, to take a bike ride with him. She aggressively responded, "I'd rather cry in a BMW than laugh on a bike" (Wang 2017; Zavoretti 2016). This illustrates the materialism of today's marriage market, exacerbated by rising class inequality and the huge cost of weddings. Wedding costs especially burden the groom's family, who must provide most of the wedding expenses, as well as buy the young couple a new house, as the residential nuclear family becomes more popular. The importance of social status in the contemporary marriage market has resulted in the growth of offline matchmaking entrepreneurs who specialize in finding ideal brides—young, thin, with long hair, very pale skin, and not too educated—for a growing class of millionaires who are willing to pay thousands of dollars to find the "perfect bride" (Larmer 2013).

Increasing costs of marriage for ordinary lower- and middle-class men have reintroduced the important financial role of parents whose sons could never afford today's wedding costs on their own. Thus, in many Chinese cities, both parents and their children still view marriage as a family affair. On weekends, urban public parks are jammed with people seeking prospective spouses for their children or themselves, an especially difficult, often heartbreaking effort for men who lost their jobs in the 2008 economic meltdown (Zavoretti 2016; Larmer 2013).

The high costs of weddings and marriage have also led to an increase in "naked marriages," which occur between partners who have few material assets. "Naked marriages" are based on the "Five Nos": no ring, no ceremony, no honeymoon, no home, and no car. While sociologists sometimes call naked marriages a "helpless choice," a couple may rather see love and wanting to be together as more important than a ceremonious, expensive wedding. Some praise naked marriages, using the rationale that "it's more important to choose the right person with whom to spend the rest of your life" (Ford 2011). Another type of coupling, called "flash marriages," takes place between couples who have known each other for less than one month.

Sometimes these marriages represent the new value placed on romantic love, but they also may be economically motivated; in both cases, they are embraced by men more than women. And in either case, they are more likely to end in divorce, which is now at 30 percent and rising (Zhi 2014).

THE INCREASING VALUE OF LOVE

The changes regarding the role of love in China became particularly dramatic to me as I remembered my Chinese calligraphy class, which I took 35 years ago. With Valentine's Day approaching, I asked my professor to help me write a card to my husband saying "I Love You" in calligraphy. "You can't do that," she said. "In China we don't celebrate Valentine's Day." That was then; this is now. Valentine's Day is widely celebrated in contemporary China, mainly defined by the Western commercial aspect of gift exchange, consistent with the current pattern of Chinese consumerism. Another festival centered on coupling and commerce is Singles Day, held on November 11. First organized in 1993 by male university students to celebrate being single, it now is an event where young men and women look for long-term romantic relationships through "Blind Date" parties. Singles Day is now the largest offline and online shopping day in the world (Stampler 2014).

With approximately 35 million more men than women in China today, the government has become concerned about social instability and criminal activities such as sex trafficking and sexual violence. Thus, they have expanded their own matchmaking activities, joining with the Communist Youth League and the All-China Women's Federation to organize mass speed dating events. Matchmaking entrepreneurs have also gained the government's approval, such as the offline Fall in Love Emotional Education school, which seeks male clients who have never dated or been in a romantic relationship. The school has experienced widespread success, and the school's leader, Ye Chaoqun, says 90 percent of his students have found girlfriends (Wee 2017). As one student said, "I think there are many single women who are just like me . . . all longing for love."

Longing for love, maybe, but longing for marriage, not quite. A significant change in contemporary China is the increasing numbers of both men and women who are resigning themselves to not getting married (FlorCruz 2015). Shareen Chang, a businesswoman in her late 20s, says that "marriage has become increasingly unappealing," citing family pressures, high costs, and the high divorce rate. Unmarried women past 25 are considered "leftover women," and their numbers are increasing (Lake 2018). The average age of marriage for women now is 27, similar to the age in the United States. "I'm in no hurry to get married," says Chang, "I want to date and fall in love and maybe . . . even want children someday, but a traditional marriage is no longer on my checklist." Chang does go on dates, which she says "are not serious but are just for fun. There's no doubt in my mind that love exists and that I want and need it, I just don't think it has anything to do with marriage."

1. Describe four major changes in traditional Chinese marriage and family practices from the imperial era until today.
2. How have women benefitted from the present marriage laws?
3. In China today, love and marriage are tightly connected to capitalism and consumerism. Describe the effects of this connection.
4. What are some major similarities and difference between love, marriage, and family in contemporary China and in the United States?

Chapter Four

Marriage and Love
Variations on a Theme in Modern India

The Hindu god Kama embodies love and sexual desire; he shoots his flower arrows from a bow made of sugar cane. . . . No one can ignore the arrows of Kama.

— The Kama Sutra of Vatsyayana,
Richard Burton, translator (1962)

Romantic love, which is central in ancient Indian literature and religion, is enacted in contemporary rituals, festivals, and the arts, including erotic sculptures in Hindu temples. Along with right conduct and obtaining material security, *kama*—desire, affection, love, lust, and sensual pleasure—is one of the essential goals of life. These are described in the ancient Indian text quoted above, which outlines specific practices to maximize sexual pleasure (Burton 1962). Many religious narratives describe these relationships: the love between Radha and the god Krishna is also a form of religious devotion. Love, however, is not the basis for Indian marriage.

LOVE MARRIAGE AND ARRANGED MARRIAGE

Marry first. Love will follow.

— Shaifali Sandhya (2009)

India's great religious, ethnic, linguistic, class, and **caste** diversity is unified by the cultural practice of arranged marriage, in which parents choose the spouse of their child. Marriage is the most critical institution shaping every Indian woman's life; marrying off one's daughter, called *kanyadan*, meaning the gift of a bride, is every family's responsibility. For women, especially, adult status is embodied in having a husband and children. Ancient texts stress that the first obligation of a woman is to respect, please, and obey her husband (Dwyer 2000). Bearing children is essential to cement a marriage, though today even maternity is affected by globalization (Donner 2009). As in the past, sons are preferred, and there is a good chance of a pregnancy ending in abortion if a female fetus is identified (Goldberg 2013; Kunzig 2011). In Hinduism's four stages of life, the stage of "the householder" refers to a married couple, whose major obligation is to marry off their children; only with the marriage and reproduction of a third generation can men and women move on to the final stages of meditation and a spiritual existence.

Love has many meanings in India (Lynch 1990). An intense cultural discussion today questions the role of love in contemporary marriages. Indians use the term "love marriage" to refer to the process whereby men and women meet on their own and choose their own mates. A love marriage is closely associated with a modern identity; it is increasingly affected by the global economy and featured in international media such as films, television, and the internet. Some contemporary India research views love marriages as creating a "domestic revolution"—causing couples to marry at later ages, splintering traditional families, increasing the number of single mothers and live-in relationships prior to marriage, increasing premarital and extramarital sex, promoting greater awareness of female sexual pleasure, leading to higher rates of divorce and remarriage for women (traditionally, divorced women did not remarry), postponing childbearing, and leading to more dual income households as women become more educated and work outside the home (Trivedi 2014; Sandhya 2009). Based on these trends, psychologist Shaifali Sandhya declares that the "Indian marriage is burning."

This chapter explores changes in Indian society related to sexuality, love, and marriage through three ethnographies: my own fieldwork among the professional and business class in Mumbai (formerly Bombay), the call-center culture of Hyderabad, and lower-class girls who work in export garment factories in Chennai (formerly Madras). These examples indicate that Indian marriage is not "burning," although it is changing. The expectations that a girl will be a virgin when she marries, and the importance of her maintaining her honor, are still very strong. In the traditional social context of female seclusion, arranged marriages, by matchmakers in the past and today by family elders, was an adaptive feature of Indian culture. Changes are emerging only gradually and are characterized more by compromises and integration of past practices than by the complete opposition to arranged and love marriages represented in some media and even in academic literature.

THE URBAN UPPER-MIDDLE CLASS OF MUMBAI: ARRANGED MARRIAGE

> Match for 31 year old girl from Panjab working at Punjab National Bank. Well educated family. 5'1". Slim, Beautiful. Only Child. Govt. or good private job. Caste no bar. (Bride Wanted 2018)

> Suitable tall, intelligent, professional girl wanted for an innocently and issuelessly divorced 35 year old boy 6'1", MS, US citizen, intelligent, handsome Software Engineer from an Army Officer family, high salary in reputed company, religion, caste no bar. (Bride Wanted 2018)

Indian arranged marriage is adapted to the importance of the extended joint family, which is (with few exceptions) patrilineal, patrilocal, and patriarchal. Caste, ethnicity, social status, educational level, religion, region of origin, and today, foreign citizenship and/or willingness to migrate are also important. Ideally, the married couple lives in the husband's household, although nuclear families are increasing, due to economically motivated migration or as a response to severe conflicts within the patrilocal family. Tradition mandates that a wife will adjust to her husband's family and subordinate her own personality, desires, and preferences to those of his parents and older siblings. If circumstances permit, all a family's sons bring their wives into the household, which is ruled over by the sons' father; mothers also play a dominant role in everyday household life. Indeed, in contemporary literature on India, household conflicts most often involve mothers-in-law and daughters-in-law (Nanda and Gregg 2009; Divakaruni 1995). Affective relations between the newly married couple are carefully scrutinized, as they can undermine a mother-in-law's power. A bride's relations with her own family are also severely regulated, as these connections, too, affect her commitment to her new family.

The site of my fieldwork was populated by professional- and business-class North Indian families in Mumbai, but ethnographic research conducted in Calcutta and Delhi illustrates many similarities (Donner and Santos 2016; Donner 2016; Donner 2009). Marriages are mainly arranged by parents through their own social networks, frequently women's social associations (Nanda 1983), or through newspaper or internet matchmaking advertisements. The "stranger marriages" of the past, where the bride and groom never meet before the wedding, rarely occur today. Rather, among contemporary upper-middle-class, urban-

Love marriages are becoming more common among the upper-middle classes of India. Prathmesh Kapoor and Pallav Ganatca are both dentists who met and fell in love in graduate school. Although they are from different ethnic groups both families approved the marriage and they had a typical luxurious Indian upper-middle-class wedding soon after they graduated.

ized, educated families, the prospective couple first meets in the presence of their parents—in supervised settings—where they can decide if they have the "right chemistry" to make a happy marriage. Later, they may talk on the phone, chat via the internet, or even go out together, though more likely in a group, as "dating" or even "moving about" on her own can jeopardize a girl's reputation. The boy or girl can refuse the offer to marry, and only then will their parents suggest a new prospect. Marriage is so essential to an individual's identity and the family's reputation, however, that at some point pressure is applied on both girls and boys to agree to an arranged match.

The bride's interaction with her husband's family follows the very complex rules of the Indian kinship system, which, for example, distinguishes between the ages of kin and their affiliation to the paternal or maternal line (Nanda 1998). This system incorporates principles of male seniority and inheritance, the lower status of the bride's family in relation to the groom's family (in order to preserve the male-centered hierarchy), the obligations of a male child to care for his parents in their old age, and an eldest son's obligation to perform specific rituals in life-cycle ceremonies such as marriage and death. The kinship rules express the cultural commitment to the importance of the family beyond the household, even for those who live abroad.

Although dowry has been illegal since 1961, it almost always accompanies an arranged marriage, whether demanded from the boy's family or framed as a "gift" from the girl's family. With the extreme consumerism among families today, dowry has become a source of conflict for upwardly mobile families. Among the lower class and rural families, the pressure on a bride's family to pay a dowry, the full amount of which may be beyond their means, sometimes results in a wife's death (dowry death). The wife might commit suicide over being harassed to pay or be murdered by her husband or in-laws for not meeting their dowry demands. Her death enables the husband to pursue a new marriage and another dowry (Hitchcock 2001). The dowry, traditionally consisting of gold jewelry, but today including automobiles and expensive household appliances, theoretically belongs to the girl after marriage; it is usually her only form of inheritance. Whatever form it takes, however, gift exchanges are always part of the typically elaborate Indian wedding ceremony, which is generally paid for by the girl's parents.

In today's arranged marriages, a "suitable" girl is judged by her ability and willingness to live in a joint family: Can she get along in an extended household? Is she "too educated" to accept subordination to her in-laws? Is she willing to circumscribe her relations with her own family? Will she complain about too many domestic chores keeping her at home? Will she resent caring for her husband's parents? Is she attractive, light skinned, not too fat, stylish? And in spite of the fact that there are more single men than women, the search for "a suitable boy" is equally demanding, focusing mainly on his professional accomplishments, earning power, and the reputation of his family (Nanda 2016; Seth 1993). As the marriage advertisements above suggest, matching age, height, profession, looks, and family background are all important. "Caste no bar" refers to the family's willingness to make a match with a person from a caste different from their own; this is usually related to some liability on the part of the son or daughter for whom the match is being sought. In the cases above, the age of the girl is a drawback, as the age of a girl when she marries is normally much younger. In the case of the boy, it is his divorce that will be a great obstacle in finding him a wife.

Despite the growing acceptance of romantic love as important in marriage, the continuing preference for arranged marriages is more widespread than is suggested in much academic and popular literature. Many nontraditional practices, such as premarital sex, are more often debated than practiced. Some young women declare, "I won't marry anyone I don't love," but the pressure to marry, especially for young women, continues to incorporate a role for the elders who still can and do wield power over the choice of a spouse. The weakening of traditional cultural elements like the importance of the extended family and of caste, class, and ethnic endogamy is somewhat overstated in popular media (Donner and Santos 2016; Donner 2016). Individual rights are enshrined in the Indian constitution, but legal codes governing inheritance, marriage, guardianship, and property remain anchored in traditional community structures, are outlined in ancient religious and legal texts, and were continued under British colonialism. While emotional ties between spouses both before and after marriage are becoming increasingly important, intergenerational ties and coresidence remain as strong commitments to what is a diverse range of changing ideas and practices. Certainly, one central reason for the persistence of arranged marriages and patrilocality, however modified, is the importance of marriage in individual and collective acts of mutual assistance that are expected to last a lifetime.

LOVE AND LOVE MARRIAGE

In the reality of Indian middle-class urban life, arranged marriages tend to accommodate family interests while at the same time endorsing companionate marriage and the love that is expected to develop over time; this is true even for many Indian migrants to the United States (Pappu 2017; Flock 2018).

A "love marriage" that is strongly opposed by parents, however, is considered very threatening to traditional family structures, especially where material interests predominate, as in concerns about upward mobility among the urban middle class (Donner and Santos 2016; Donner 2016). With the modern identity of individualism gaining credibility, however, the lines between arranged and love marriages are blurring. In the past, families were more knowledgeable about each other's history, but with urban migration intense "research" is needed to assure confidence in a family's suitability; this may even include using a private detective.

Globalization is also significantly affecting marriage, particularly in workspaces that depend on women employees, such as international call centers and garment export factories. New ideas regarding sex, love, and marriage are not overthrowing traditional marital practices, but they are, however gradually, creating a culture of change.

SITES OF CHANGE: INTERNATIONAL CALL CENTERS

Call centers have become important additions to cities like Hyderabad, juxtaposing the ancient and the modern, having emerged in the wake of the information technology boom of the 1990s. These call centers employ English-speaking male and female college students and recent college graduates both from Hyderabad and from other Indian cities (Kapur 2010). This business environment offers radically new opportunities for mixed socializing that leads young people to reframe their ideas about sex, love, marriage, and divorce. Although highly attractive to upwardly mobile young people, the centers pose problems for traditional Indian culture: Women working in call centers do not need to rely as much on family and kin for financial and social support within the family residence; tight social control over women's activities is weakened.

In contrast to most professional Indian workplaces, over 60 percent of Hyderabad call-center employees are women, requiring many of the centers to reconfigure their operations, often under pressure from the employees' parents. Single-sex break rooms have been created; transportation facilities include increased security; and dormitory living has become more popular, partly because many local landlords refuse to rent to women for fear that these private apartments will become sites of dating and sexual relations. Most female call-center employees enjoy their jobs, both for the ability to earn their own living and for the freedom to meet and socialize with new friends of both sexes. Traditional values about safeguarding a girl's reputation are still powerful, however, so most girls date in a group, try to get appointed to the same shifts of the boys they are interested in, and use their cell phones to chat and arrange to meet, rather than date as a couple. The cell phone is probably one of the most important technological changes enabling this new social atmosphere, not just in India, but in other cultures as well, as noted in the chapter on the Igbo.

Increased socializing between the sexes in call centers and other urban spaces raise questions among Indians of different generations about whether the traditional pattern of arranged marriage can be sustained: the answer appears to be a definite yes. As one young woman call-center worker indicated, although she likes dating boys from work, she will probably depend on her parents to find her a husband, because she does not know the families of the boys she works with, and thus "cannot know for sure who is truly a good match" (Kapur 2010:54). Many of the young call-center workers also note that the informal dating of the call center puts off the stressful decision regarding marriage and prevents them from "jumping into impulsive [love] marriages." As another example, one young man whose aging parents needed intensive medical care declared, "I am the only son . . . I [do] meet many girls at work but I told my parents, 'please pick someone whom you will get along well with because she will be here taking care of you at night while I am at work.'" Despite what might seem to be a burden to a bride in the United States, the young man's

Indian call centers, where men and women work together, are a new source of sociability, which is considered risky in undermining the Indian pattern of arranged marriage.

position, prominently mentioned in his matrimonial advertisement, attracted a plethora of women. But call-center women workers are not always considered desirable, and some matrimonial advertisements specify that "girls who work at international call centers need not apply," perhaps because they are viewed as too liberated or would not spend sufficient time on their domestic responsibilities.

Although today, concerns about the happiness of the conjugal couple may supersede the interests of the family, it is widely understood that "love marriages" can be risky. Where there is intense family hostility, a young couple in a love marriage is cut off from the family companionship and financial help so crucial in the early stages of a marriage in this social class. Occasionally, the family will declare the couple dead, although sometimes reconciliation occurs when a child is born. A serious problem for young women is that a man who enters into a love marriage is more likely to abandon his wife after a few years because the kin group has no hold over him and no dowry has been paid.

Divorce, which is almost always blamed on the woman, remains stigmatized and burdensome, though its greater acceptance is indicated by the emergence of online matchmaking websites specifically aimed at divorcees. While it is clear that call centers have affected the ideas of the younger generation regarding love and marriage, it is not clear how fast or how much effect they will have on future realities.

SITES OF CHANGE: INDIAN GARMENT FACTORIES

We are now new women.

— Female garment factory worker, quoted in Lessinger (2013)

In her aptly titled ethnographically-based article, "Love and Marriage in the Shadow of the Sewing Machine," anthropologist Johanna Lessinger examines how the small-scale garment export manufacturers who flocked to Chennai in the 1970s made a huge impact on traditional cultural patterns involving gender roles, love, marriage, and family. By the 1990s, the factory labor force, which previously employed few women, was overwhelmingly young and female. In the past, sending unmarried daughters out to work lowered a family's status by exposing girls to "dangerous outsiders" and the temptations of sex. Today, due to rising consumer prices, residence dislocation through gentrification, and increasing under- and unemployment for boys and men, sending daughters to work in the garment factories is often an economic necessity. Thus, even a low-paying factory job transformed a young, unmarried girl, traditionally the most peripheral member of her family, into the household's major breadwinner. This placed new financial and moral burdens on a girl, and although it did not substantially increase her power in the family, it provided social opportunities beyond the traditional seclusion of her home and neighborhood. Factory work immersed a girl in a wider world of choices, including the choice of a spouse. Some young female factory workers say they do not want to marry at all, but others save their salaries for a future dowry, bypassing the financial role of their elders in arranging their marriages and thus increasing their own autonomy.

From a family's point of view, the idea that a girl is likely to find love in the social context of the factory is the most threatening aspect of her job; an emotional relationship with someone not chosen by parents flouts parental authority, compromises family status and honor, and overturns the possibility of an advantageous family alliance. As in call centers, factory owners are aware of these problems and, in the interest of keeping open the supply of local, single female workers, attempt, not always successfully, to avoid opportunities for male–female relationships by segregating the sexes in work areas and hiring males only as supervisors.

THE EFFECTS OF POVERTY ON ARRANGED MARRIAGE

However much poor families say they prefer arranged marriages, however, they cannot always do this successfully, nor can they organize the lavish weddings that are still integral to Indian culture. Poor families who do not successfully arrange the marriage of their daughters are often criticized, sometimes for negligence, or perhaps because, as one critic of such families said, "A garment girl is the goose laying the golden egg. The family won't let her go." Arranging her own "love" marriage is a way out for a young woman, who may elope, marry in a registry office, or simply declare herself married. And while families cling to the idea of caste endogamy and potential upward class mobility through "good" marriages, many in the younger generation appear to have discarded these ideas. And occasionally a love marriage works out well.

But, alas, love more often fails, leading to great sorrow, mainly for the woman; men may pretend to be in love to have sex, but even if they marry for love, they frequently abandon their wives. If this happens after the wife gets pregnant, she has only two choices: an abortion or raising the child on her own without any family support. Divorce is always a serious choice because women on their own, especially those who are separated or divorced from a love marriage, are more subject to sexual assaults.

The many love marriages Lessinger describes among garment factory girls suggest ambiguity, contradictions, and complexity and require a cautious evaluation of the role of globalization in improving women's status. On the one hand, new employment opportunities increase women's earning power, give them the right to move outside the home, create new social relationships, widen the arena of autonomy, and help form a modern identity. On the other hand, a love marriage may lead to separation from kin, abandonment, and a loss of honor and status, with only a short-term emotional gain and subsequent loneliness and desperation.

Love marriages are clearly accelerating the Indian trend toward nuclear families and weakened kinship ties, particularly among the urban lower classes, but they have not guaranteed gender equality within marriage. For those women who are determined to press on with their newfound autonomy, a love marriage can be life changing; for the others, who are in the majority, a successful arranged marriage perhaps offers greater advantages, particularly if it turns into a companionate relationship that provides security, honor, children, and ultimately, one hopes, love.

1. What are some of the advantages and disadvantages in an arranged marriage for the husband? For the wife?
2. Would you consider an arranged marriage for yourself? Refer to the chapter in giving your reasons.
3. How do "love marriages" threaten the Indian family?
4. Referring to the chapter, explain how social class affects love marriages.

Chapter Five

Sexuality, Love, and Marriage
The Brazilian Favela

"They want a woman to stay in the house, hidden," Marta said, referring to husbands. "He [my husband] won't let me out of the house alone. . . . He would kill me if I gave him horns [cheat on him]. And I don't want to die."

— Jessica Gregg (2006)

This chapter examines sexuality, love, gender relations, and marriage in the Brazilian *favela*, or shantytown, and how these patterns have been shaped by Portuguese colonialism, the cultural pattern of honor and shame, the role of race in intimate relationships, and the effect of poverty on gender roles.

PORTUGUESE COLONIZATION

The first Portuguese sailors to reach Brazil, in 1500, were enchanted by the exotic "Paradise" they discovered, where the indigenous native women "were comely, naked, and without shame." During the first century of colonization, the indigenous population began dying out largely due to European diseases. The lack of native slave labor to work sugar plantations established by the Portuguese led them import slaves from Africa. In colonial times, with marriageable white women in short supply, white men took indigenous Indian women and later African or mixed-blood women as sexual partners, though rarely in formal church marriages. These unions resulted in a large mixed-blood (mulatto) population, indicating the importance of sexuality as a key to the creation of a multiracial, hierarchical, and patriarchal society, which is the foundation of contemporary Brazil (Skidmore 2009).

In the colonial patriarchal family the patriarch, his European wife, and his legitimate children lived together in the plantation's "big house"; a second "family" consisted of mistresses, illegitimate children, slaves, and tenant farmers. The patriarch had absolute control over both families and enforced his authority by the frequent use of his legal right to invoke violence.

Colonial gender relations defined men as superior, strong, virile, and active, and women as inferior and weak, and legitimately subject to a man's domination. This opposition justified a moral double standard in which men had complete freedom in sexual relations, while women's sexual pleasure was linked to the obligation to conceive and raise children. The patriarch strictly controlled the sexual activities of both his wife and his mistresses. For example, under colonial law a husband, suspecting or discovering a wife's adultery, could kill her and the adulterer, because the murders were considered to be a legitimate defense of the husband's honor. As a result, upper-class women turned into virtual recluses, seldom venturing out of the house, even to attend church (Skidmore 2009). While much has changed, this colonial culture continues to influence contemporary Brazilian society. Right up until the present, violence against women remains part of the gender dynamic requiring women to be subservient. The full spectrum of gender-based violence includes domestic battering, sexual exploitation, honor killings, and rape (Barbara 2017; Hautzinger 2007).

HONOR, SHAME, AND THE PATRIARCHAL BARGAIN

Underlying the colonial pattern of gender relations was the Portuguese sexual ideology of honor and shame, central to all Mediterranean cultures. This ideology defined women in terms of their sexual behavior, which was controlled by her parents (and after she married, became the responsibility of her husband). A woman's status was directly linked to her sexual purity, and her impurity was linked to shame. Honor was essentially a male domain and derived from a man's ability to guard and control a woman's purity. The Catholic Church played a significant role in reinforcing these attitudes, focusing on female status as achieved through sexual restraint, preservation of virginity, and marriage (Gregg 2006).

A woman assumed the proper role of wife and mother that required her to be faithful to her husband. A man who lost control over a woman's sexuality became a cuckold (*corno*); his honor was sullied and his masculinity questioned (Parker 2009). The man's role required continuous public demonstrations of masculinity through dress, comportment, speech, affect, and virility. In this cultural pattern, the emphasis is less on "being a good man," than "being good at being a man" (Gilmore 1987:4, 16).

The hierarchal opposition between masculinity and femininity also applied to male and female genitalia. The slang for male genitalia placed emphasis on the active, aggressive, and powerful nature of the phallus, symbolizing it as a weapon for violence and violation and also in terms of its potency and creative power. Linguistic terms for female genitalia symbolized it as both the object of violence and paradoxically a source of danger, linked to bodily impurities, uncleanliness, pollution, and contamination, and evoked a sense of inferiority, incompleteness, and passivity (Parker 2009).

This basic distinction between active masculinity and passive femininity carries over to the sex act itself. Penetration in intercourse implies an act of control, domination, and conquest (Kulick 1998). The masculine value on virility and the identification of femininity with fertility underlay male and female gender roles. *Macho* embodies force and power, violence and aggression, virility, and sexual potency, in bed and in the street. It contrasts with *viado* (literally, a deer, the most delicate and fragile of animals), an individual who takes the passive role in sex, as well as one who is considered a corno. Both viado and corno are applied to men who fail to live up to the macho ideal (Parker 2009). A virgin woman is defined as a maiden or even a little saint; a woman who loses her virginity outside of marriage is classified as a whore, someone who has dishonored her whole family.

These opposing masculine and feminine ideals are incorporated into children's socialization. Young girls ideally remain at home and are largely kept ignorant about sexuality and intercourse. Boys, after the age of six, play outside the home in same-sex groups, which exchange sexual information and often initiate sexual activity. In a boy's socialization, nothing is more important than stamping out passivity.

ECONOMICS AND THE PATRIARCHAL BARGAIN

Dear Authorities I just don't know what to do
With so much violence I fear living
Because I live in a favela I get no respect
There sadness and happiness walk side by side.

— Julio Rasta/Kátia, quoted in Goldstein (2013)

The honor/shame complex described above is intricately linked to economics as part of the "patriarchal bargain" in which male support and protection of women are exchanged for control of female sexuality and the appropriation of women's labor and their children (Gregg 2006; Kandiyoti 1988). This bargain became incredibly difficult as Brazil's source of labor shifted away from agriculture. Growing competition from European sugar growers and increasing industrialization severely deflated the early prosperity of agricultural Brazil, reducing the need for peasant labor and increasing rural migration to cities, leading to the rapid growth of favelas. Most men who migrated to cities could not get permanent jobs, however, and ended up working in the informal economy, for example by hiring themselves out on an irregular basis to whatever businesses would employ them. These shantytowns were wretchedly poor, with no schools, no health clinics, no garbage pickup, no paved roads, and no sewage system. In the favelas, men had difficulty supporting their families, so women had to take on wage labor to support themselves and their children. For women, the most common employment opportunity was poorly paid domestic work with no legal government benefits or protections. This role reversal weakened the traditional male–female bonds. Although marriage was broadly defined as including any relationship involving both sexual activity and moderate to long-term financial support, the bargain only worked when men had sufficient resources to support women and their children.

While most men prefer that their wives stay home performing domestic labor, this is difficult when men cannot find decent employment. In cities, it has been easier for women than men to find employment: working as domestics, babysitting, sewing goods at home, or working in factories, earning an income closer to that of men. A poor woman is motivated to find a job and substantially contribute to the family income and thus less likely to continue to be economically dependent on a man (Rebhun 1999a). Because men's relationships with their children extend from their affiliation with their children's mothers, they find it easier to abandon the child along with the mother. A man can always find another woman to do housework and to fulfill his sexual demands, while a woman with many children becomes a burden. Thus, the patriarchal bargain begins to crumble, affecting both the ideal and the reality of intimate relationships.

Life expectancy in the favelas, especially for infants and children, is very low, and because women must work, any child not in school is also expected to find work (Kenny 2007). Babies are simply left at home alone, with the door securely fastened; thus many ill babies die alone and unattended. As anthropologist Nancy Scheper-Hughes describes in her heartbreaking ethnography, many mothers who saw their very ill infants as fated to die stepped back and allowed nature to take its course (1993; 2013). When Scheper-Hughes once attempted to help a sick toddler whose mother totally ignored him, women in the favela derided the anthropologist's attempt to "fight with death." The ideology of the Catholic Church that condemns both contraception and abortion (which is still illegal), and the general absence of public pediatric health care facilities, further contributes to the early deaths of poor children.

LOVE DESIRED, LOVE ABANDONED

In the rural agrarian economy, the idea of "love" mainly applied to kin and friends and was enacted through the exchange of material resources and services within a close social network. With respect to men, older rural women characterize love as labor; it is what each partner does for the other: the husband brings home a paycheck, the woman cooks, cleans the house, and "services" (has sex with) her husband. Sex is like other household tasks, not a transformative intimate relationship. Love means the partners carry out their obligations with consideration as part of a long-term relationship. It takes on the qualities of mother-love: self-abnegating, suffering, generous, something that no man feels required to do (Rebhun 1999a).

The combination of economic instability and the failure of male protection has led some women in the favela to abandon the idea of love and monogamous marriage altogether. They define themselves outside of the prevailing sexual ideology, preferring freedom, or *liberdade* (liberty). These women believe that guarding their virginity in order to marry well is an outdated notion and it is more important to do what they want to do without being under a man's control. They have little faith in a man providing security, holding that "he may help for a while, but then he is gone" (Gregg 2006:164). As a woman who worked as a maid told the ethnographic interviewer, she was satisfied with her relatively reliable source of income with no one to "step on her foot and control her."

Some of these women hold bitter feelings toward men and see sex as a means of vengeance. Few women express love for their partner, and some deny that love exists in the favela. Married women often say they do not love their husbands but are just used to each other. They believe that a man who does not protect and provide for them has lost the right to be loved and trusted. When asked about a man she just married one woman said that she likes him a lot but doesn't love him, and defined love as the emotion you feel for your mother or sisters.

In spite of widespread desire for love among younger couples, the major drawback to lasting companionate marriage in the favela is the dire poverty and the inability of men to find work.

Many women, especially those who suffered violence in their marriages, saw men as aggressive and humiliating. Another woman declared, "It's better to work than to break your head over men who just want to exploit you. I want to live alone and just have a man when I really need one, like they do with us" (Gregg 2006:167).

Married women are almost never unfaithful, but women who choose liberty often flaunt multiple partners; indeed one of their aims is to make cuckolds of men, upending the unstated rules of favela gender relations. "This is a war," one woman said, meaning that cuckolding a man was not just about getting him to uphold his part of the patriarchal bargain, but it was also a protest against infidelity as a male right. Unfortunately, this resistance has little cultural consequence because it does not attack the root causes of the problem of living in an economy that cripples male earning power, encourages male mobility, and makes transitory sexual relationships the norm. Can liberdade ultimately change the economic structure, or will it just bring equal-opportunity misery? That is the question.

In the favelas, despite all the economic hardships, however, the younger generation considers love as meaning something different than it did in the past. Young women in the favelas today are influenced by popular films and television, and daydream of an exciting companion whom they will love and marry. Today romantic love is increasingly embraced as part of intimate gender relationships. Unfortunately, the failure of young dreamers to consider economic realities often leads to the breakup of marriages. While the Biblical view that mixing emotional love with economic considerations sullies love's purity, the pressure for economic survival within the severe poverty in the favela makes economic considerations necessary (Rebhun 1999b). For some women, mainly light-skinned mulattos, one path to social mobility or a way out of the favela, is to seduce an older, richer, whiter man, hoping to obtain long-term economic sustenance or in a "more extreme happy ending," move into his apartment (Goldstein 2013:154).

Today, there is greater freedom for daughters and some changes about ideas of respectability. This has encouraged some men to attach discourses of passion and romance to marriage and pseudo-marriage with "decent" women and allows young women to dream of love that is both exciting and respectable. Influenced by a global media, this more privatized, romanticized, and eroticized concept of love within the conjugal bond is growing among the younger generation. There is now a greater expectation of personal attachment before marriage or cohabitation and the beginnings of a shift in emphasis from the mother–child bond to the conjugal bond as the primary affective tie.

OBSTACLES TO CHANGE

Despite changes embraced by the younger generation, traditional ideas remain: the distinction between the women's secluded domain "of the house" and the male domain "of the street" still influences the moral world. Sexual virtue still defines women in the favela, and the principal accusation against a deviant woman is that she is a whore. This gender model prevents women from living alone because such women, who are neither virgins, coupled, nor mothers, are sexually suspect; their families will still pressure them into marriage to save their honor. Favela women continue to believe that girls must maintain their virginity and be faithful to their spouses. Mothers "imprison" daughters in their house so that men can't seduce them and "take their value." An adolescent girl who loses her virginity outside of marriage has no value, no one respects her (Rebhun 1999a:59). Thus, even if a man is abusive, "a house without a man is terrible" (Gregg 2006:160).

Younger urban men speak of love as infatuation or passion while women think it more important that a man verbally declares his love for them. In the past, romantic passion was viewed as both extramarital and tragic, while marital love was a calm routine. This changed as the Western idea of romantic love as the basis of marriage became more accepted. Older women see male infidelity more as a "vulgar irritation" than a serious threat to the marriage as long as the husband does not give the "other" woman material goods, father children with her, or buy her a house. But for younger couples who view marriage as based on passionate love, and sexual intercourse as "making love," extramarital sex is a threat even when the man is not materially involved with his extramarital partner.

The contemporary pressure to verbalize love presents a serious problem for men, who regard such outward statements about their feelings as effeminate. A man may feel compelled to father as many children as possible to prove his virility while a woman may strive to have a man's baby in an attempt to gain his support. As a result of these role pressures men often drink heavily, womanize ostentatiously, and commit violence, while women suffer emotional illnesses, often in the form of spirit possession (Rebhun 1999a). Still, some women hold on to the hope that one day they will achieve true love.

RACE, CLASS, AND SEXUALITY

Brazilians frequently express concepts of love in terms of temperature, describing themselves as "hot-blooded," and therefore passionate both emotionally and sexually. This identity incorporates long-held racialized concepts such as the greater sensuality attributed to African people of the Tropics. Hot-bloodedness is most commonly applied to the Brazilian lower classes and darker skinned people: the mulatta, or mixed race woman, is exalted as exotic, sexually appealing, and desirable (Rebhun 1999a; Hindert 2016).

After 1888, when Brazil abolished slavery, government policy attempted to "whiten" its population by encouraging European immigration and teaching only European-centered history and culture (Goldstein 2013). Today, individuals with African ancestry account for about 45 percent of Brazil's total population. Most define themselves not as *preta* (black) but rather as *parda*, or brown, indicating partial African ancestry. Brazilian understandings of race are diverse and flexible; there is no legal racial discrimination, but race is implicated in a profoundly unequal class system: whites at the top, blacks at the bottom, and parda somewhere in-between. The Brazilian racial continuum consists of multiple categories, and most people identify themselves in an intermediate category between black and white, and racially identify others depending on their social class.

Government policy now views multiracialism positively and as central to Brazil's national identity as a racial democracy. This perspective, however, does not mean that racial discrimination and racial stratification are nonexistent, as racial inequality exacts a high toll. On every measure of social and economic well-being, Brazilians who self-identify as having African ancestry are far worse off than those who self-identify as white: their illiteracy rates are far higher and their wages are far lower, with higher education almost exclusively found among white Brazilians. As one Brazilian told a reporter, "Black is Beautiful, but White—White is just Easier" (Nolen 2015).

The intertwining of sexuality, race, class, and gender in Brazil is most evident in **Carnival** (a Brazilian festival that marks the beginning of Lent) and **samba** (a sensual Brazilian dance of African origin), central features of Brazilian culture for both Brazilians and outsiders (Ickes 2013). The declining influence of conservative Catholicism and growing fragmentation of the family have led to an increased focus on the legitimacy of sexual pleasure. This legitimacy is mainly incorporated into marginalized, stigmatized subcultures such as those of prostitutes, gays, self-styled bohemians, and youth, but is also prominently displayed in Carnival and samba. Carnival, particularly, overturns the hierarchical, patriarchal and puritanical structure of the ordinary world by its highly sexualized performances and its mingling of people from different classes and subcultures. This inversion of the class system transforms the poorest favela inhabitants into kings and queens. In Carnival, work and the suffering of daily life give way to a world of laughter, when the normal conditions of human existence,

The intertwining of sexuality, race, class, and gender is most evident in the ritual of Carnival, in which the mulatta, the sexual symbol of Carnival, becomes the symbol of Brazil itself.

marked by almost overwhelming sadness, are transformed into the happiness and joy of the festival.

Carnival and samba both feature African elements, particularly in music and dance (Parker 2009; Sims 2018). The mulatta, the sexual symbol of Carnival, becomes the representation of Brazil itself. Samba also, with its sexual choreography, challenges bourgeois morality, presenting a sexuality that is primitive, savage, tropical, reckless, and unruly, playing on the whole set of white notions of black sensuality. Carnival and samba continue the separation between the street and the home. The street is the place where danger lurks, but also the place of the exuberant celebration of life. The home is the site of convention and hierarchy, in terms of both gender and power.

But just as Carnival and samba represent change in Brazil, other changes are occurring as a result of globalization (Kottak 2006); greater government investment in health care and social services, both for children and victims of AIDS (Scheper-Hughes 2013); greater political participation of women locally and nationally; a more liberated religious theology (Neuhouser 1989); and more cultural participation in traditionally male cultural activities (Sims 2018).

Women generally are benefitting from these changes, but women in the favelas have a long way to go before they achieve economic parity with men and protection from male violence. Research indicates that higher levels of education make a difference for both men and women regarding gender equality and less restrictive sexuality (Heilborn and Cabral 2013). Thus, in spite of many changes, traditional Brazilian culture regarding sexuality, love, marriage, and gender is still strong, and despite modernization, much of the colonial ideology remains in place.

1. Describe three aspects of the honor/shame complex in Brazil.
2. Discuss how poverty affects love and marriage in the favela.
3. What roles do race and class play in Brazilian history and contemporary culture, particularly regarding sexuality, love, and marriage?
4. What are the major gender stereotypes in Brazil? How do these empower men and degrade women?

Chapter Six

Diversity in Islam
Exploring the Islamic Republic of Iran

This chapter discusses Islam with regard to sexuality, love, marriage, and gender roles and then examines the revolutionary changes that have taken place in the Islamic Republic of Iran. Islam is a global religion, with 1.8 billion followers in over 20 Muslim-majority nations in the Middle East, Central and Southeast Asia, Africa, and in Muslim minority nations in Europe and North America. Ninety percent of Muslims are Sunnis; the rest, including most Muslims in Iran, are Shiites. The split between the two rests on an ancient debate over who should lead Islam after the Prophet Muhammad's death in 632 (Harney 2016). Shiites say the Prophet's cousin and son-in-law, Imam Ali, should be considered as the Prophet's true successor, and Sunnis say the Prophet's trusted friends Abu Bakr, Omar, and Othman should take Muhammad's place. Despite the differing beliefs in who the Prophet's successor was, for all Muslims, the major sources of Islamic belief and practices are the Qur'an, the book revealed to the Prophet Muhammad, and the Hadith, Muhammad's commentaries. Partly because there is no central religious authority in Islam, the religion is characterized by diversity, debate, and change, rooted in historical conflicts, current national and international politics, the expanding use of international media and communication technologies, increasing education, and the spread of Islam beyond the Middle East.

The diverse, contemporary, often negative reactions to Islam in Western nations are shaped by the expansion of Islamic fundamentalism, acts of Islamic terrorists, and cultural conflicts. These conflicts center on the appropriate role of religion in state law and issues regarding sexuality and gender intensified by the expanding Islamic diaspora to Europe and the Western hemisphere (Kristoff and WuDunn 2009). Western beliefs about Muslim sexuality rest on contradictory stereotypes: on the one hand, a perception of a perverse and excessive sexuality based on colonial European illustrations of the North African harem (Alloula 1986; Nanda and Warms 2018:212–213), and on the other hand, a Western belief in Islam's oppression of women based on issues such as veiling, female circumcision, and honor killings (Abu-Lughod 2017; Wikan 2008).

WOMEN'S MODESTY

The Mediterranean honor and shame complex, which predates Islam, is widespread in the Muslim world. Islam holds that women's sexuality embodies danger and chaos, which largely accounts for the Muslim justification of strict male control over women's lives and behavior. This view underscores the role that women's modesty and virginity play in demonstrating a man's honor in Muslim societies (Mernissi 2011). "Because honor is associated with men and seen as their responsibility to own and protect on behalf of the family, women are simply an embodiment of men's honor and only serve as a potential threat to that honor and a possible trigger for chaos and dishonor" (Barry 2016).

Current debates over women's modesty focus on female dress worn in public, mainly the *hijab*, or headscarf (Zoepf 2016; Mahdavi 2015; El Feki 2013), but also, in Europe, the face veil (*burqa*) and the full-body covering worn by Muslim women at the beach (*burkini*) (Rubin 2016). The Qur'an states that "believing women . . . should lower their gaze and guard their modesty . . . [and] they should draw their veils over their bosoms and not display their beauty except to their husbands." It also speaks of erecting a curtain in order to conceal women from men's gaze (Qur'an 24:30–31). For some Muslims, this requires sex segregation in private and public; for others, it means women must wear clothing that conceals their bodies. The Qur'an requires a face covering only for Muhammad's wife, but many Muslims interpret this as requiring all women to do the same in public.

The practices regarding modest female dress vary in Muslim nations and among social classes, rural and urban populations, age groups, and cultures: they range from the total body coverings (*abaya*) and face veils required in Yemen, to the air hostesses on United Arab Emirate airplanes, who wear "jaunty little caps with attached gauzy scarves that hint at *hijab*" (Zoepf 2008). Appropriate modest dress for women is a political issue in Egypt, where almost 90 percent of Egyptian

Throughout the Islamic world, including Iran, covering the female body is an essential cultural value.

women wear a headscarf, though some government officials oppose this custom. Previously, Egyptian Bedouin women wore neither a veil nor a hijab, but more are adopting this conservative dress to assert their Muslim identity (Abu-Lughod 1999/1986). In Tunisia, as more women work outside the home, and income from the tourist industry is of great economic importance, wearing the veil is widely debated. In Turkey, the headscarf was not permitted in government offices or universities, but this is changing as Turkey becomes more conservative (Tavernise 2008). The 2018 reelection of the religiously conservative prime minister of Turkey, Recep Tayyip Erdogăn, is likely to sustain these practices. In Saudi Arabia, where full body covering was mandated, the new, moderate leader, Crown Prince Mohammed bin Salman, has permitted Saudi women to participate in an international chess tournament without wearing the abaya. In the early to mid-twentieth century, many Middle Eastern women followed Western fashions, but today some younger, educated women choose to wear the hijab in public to establish their Muslim identity (Fernea 2003); some of the younger Muslim women resent the West's "fixation" on the headscarf, which is for many Westerners the main symbol of Islam's oppression of women.

MARRIAGE AND LOVE

Islamic marriage formally requires a legal contract freely consented to by both the bride and groom, signed by a guardian of the bride, usually her father or a male relative, and two Muslim witnesses. Divorce is permitted, and though ideally requires the consent of both husband and wife, in reality, it is mainly the husband's prerogative. A man is limited to four wives, though in fact, hardly 2 percent of Muslim men worldwide practice polygyny (Ahmed 2009). Bride-price is forbidden, but the groom's family gives the bride material goods or cash, which is hers to keep. Sexuality, fidelity, companionship, and reproduction are all highly valued within marriage (Musallam 1983), and virginity is officially required for both men and women, although more rigorously controlled for women (Mahdavi 2015). In many Islamic communities, on a girl's wedding night, proof of her virginity is required by the display of bloody garments or bedding. Islamic law requires that a husband protect and support his family according to his means, and a wife's duty is to safeguard her husband's possessions and fulfill her domestic duties. A man is forbidden to beat his wife severely, and then only for a serious breach of behavior such as infidelity (Ahmed 2009).

Romantic love—longing, attraction, desire—is celebrated in Islamic poetry, but even now, arranged marriage (preferably between paternal **parallel cousins**) rather than love marriages, are the norm, and love primarily refers to the affection associated with extended family relations. As we see below, romantic love as a basis for marriage is increasing among young people in the Arabic Middle East (Davis and Davis 1995). Research also indicates that deep romantic love and companionate marriage patterns do grow over time in many Muslim marriages. This emerging pattern is keeping couples together, even overcoming the inability to have children, which is commonly blamed on the wife (Inhorn 2007). Islamic personal law, however, can work against strong, loving marriages due to relatively easy divorce, especially for men; the legality of polygyny; and the absence of communal property (Charrad 2001:35).

CHANGING IDEOLOGY AND PRACTICES IN IRAN

The Islamic Revolution is not about fun; it is about morality;
In fact there is no fun to be had in the Islamic Republic.

— Ayatollah Ruhollah Khomeini, Supreme Leader of the Islamic Republic of Iran (1980; quoted in Mahdavi 2007)

The Islamic Republic of Iran, ruled by **sharia** (Islamic) **law**, has a complex history regarding its commitment to Islamic practice. Following the 1979 Islamic Revolution that overthrew the Shah of Iran, who had been strongly supported by the United States, Iran changed from a relatively moderate Islamic nation infused with many Western values to one ruled by conservative Islamic clerics who imposed a strict Islamic lifestyle on Iranian men and women. This includes bans on the consumption of alcohol, contact with nonfamily members of the opposite sex prior to marriage, music and dancing, and wearing Westernized clothing. These rules are enforced by the "morality police" (*komite*), both in public and in private homes, and can entail harassment, jailing, and violent punishment. Since the revolution, Iranian women are required to wear the hijab and outer garments loosely covering their entire body in public.

But as Iranian-American anthropologist Pardis Mahdavi describes in *Passionate Uprisings: Iran's Sexual Revolution* (2009), in the last 20 years, beneath Iran's official Islamic policies, there is a growing underground subculture supported by young people in the urban, educated, middle- and upper-middle classes. This subculture is marked by startling changes in marital and premarital heterosocial and heterosexual relationships, which defy Islamic ideology and law. In contrast to Ayatollah Khomeini's pronouncement that the Islamic Republic is not about fun, young people are determined to have fun in many ways forbidden in the past. Much of this subculture takes place in private and depends on the black market for the purchase of alcohol, drugs, Western clothing, CDs, and movies banned by the state. It is also enabled by the widespread use of social media and the internet and is slowly moving into public space. Most recently, women have defied Iranian law by removing their headscarves in public and waving them on poles as a symbol of their refusal to accede to government restrictions (Siamdoust 2018).

These revolutionary young people are challenging Iran's Islamic culture by wearing "bad" Islamic clothing: for women, form-fitting overcoats, open-toed shoes, rolled-up pants revealing ankles, and loose head coverings with strands of dyed blond hair flowing from beneath them, lipstick, and mascara. Young men sport collarless T-shirts, shorts, gel on long locks of hair, and imported US brand-name sneakers. At private parties, young people drink alcohol, dance to the background noise of satellite TV, and even have sexual relations, including intercourse (Mahdavi 2009).

Government Responses

The government is slowly adapting to this new revolution. By the 1990s, with the support of the mayor of Tehran (who resigned in 2018), young people began to meet in public places such as parks, malls, coffee shops, pizza parlors, food courts, fast-food restaurants, video shops, and internet cafes. They attend dance classes, spas, and gyms (men and women on different days) and participate in mixed-sex hiking and sports groups with little harassment. Young Tehranis now often date, alone or in groups, and are together in cars or restaurants. Laws punishing this mixing by lashings, and imprisonment, and the death penalty for adultery are still on the books but are rarely enforced, and komite surveillance has weakened considerably. Part of this sexual revolution includes open discussions of Islamic ideas about sexual relations. The government has also expanded free public education and employment opportunities for women, which has made a significant difference in women's lives as well as in the intermingling of the sexes.

Seventy percent of Iranians are under 30 years old, and many of the urban young people are skeptical of, disaffected from, or openly hostile to the values and practices of their religious state. This is evidenced by widespread public protests throughout Iran (Erdbrink 2018). In the past, attempts by young Iranians to express their aspirations and criticisms were met with state suppression, sometimes violent, and many of younger generation decided political activism was largely useless. For this reason, they now characterize their changing social and sexual behavior as part of a wider revolution that they hope will be more effective. This revolution is also aimed at changing conversations about sex and attacking the fabric of government-determined morality, and it is setting a trend for young people beyond Tehran.

To the previous distinction in Iran between a "bad girl" or woman who sleeps around and a "good" and proper woman who saves herself for her husband, there has now been added a third category of a "normal" or "healthy" young woman who may have had one or two boyfriends before marriage, especially if she was "in love." Youthful dating is now considered acceptable, even to the parental generation, a change caused by the expansion of an online youth culture; the increasing number of women in the public sphere due to their opportunities to receive an education and work outside the home; the spread of women socializing in public places; and changes in expectations of sexual behavior (Mahdavi 2009).

The New Culture

This new culture also has rules, however: heterosocial mixing begins in groups; gradually, as people meet more frequently, flirting and showing interest slowly develop and eventually a couple may begin dating. Young women distinguish between men they are interested in primarily for sex—men who are outside their normal social circles—and a dating partner who is considered as a possibility for marriage. Even urban elite and middle-class men do not want to marry girls they have slept with, or who have slept with their friends, and

Young women socializing in public, wearing Western clothing and a loose hijab, is central to the current revolutionary culture in Iran.

girls want to avoid getting a reputation as a "slut." Because an elite girl wants to retain the respect of a man she is dating, sexual relations become complicated. Girls often play hard to get with boys who are marriage prospects, and because these boys have often spent little time with girls except for their sisters, this "play" may confuse them.

Courting in private is still the rule, but courting in public has become more common, and some girls even bring their boyfriends home to meet their families. Private courting may make opportunities for sex easier, but it also presents difficulties. As one young man said, "If you want to have sex [with an Iranian girl] you must get involved with her emotions. She may ask, 'do you love me, are you going to marry me?' For the girl it is first engagement, then sex, then love" (Mahdavi 2009:143.) This works against men who first want to have sex and then make the decision to marry. It makes them feel trapped, and so they move slowly. Men claim that women are only interested in a man's economic power and his social status, as demonstrated by his display of "cool" Western brand-name items like his shoes, watch, car, and sunglasses.

Although a girl's virginity is still highly valued, many young girls say their family's attitude is more "don't ask, don't tell," than the severe punishments of the past. Today, a girl's concern is how a potential husband will act if he finds out she is not a virgin; most young men say that virginity is not necessary but it is still a preference. Some men say it is acceptable to marry a nonvirgin, and while men may prefer a virgin, they also want a wife with some sexual experience. Dilemmas regarding sexuality are also compounded by the later age of marriage. The age of marriage is later for women, due to increasing number of women entering higher education and participating in the workforce, and also for men, due to the depressed economy, which affects their ability to get a good job. With the average age of marriage at 26 for women and 30 for men, there is a desire to have premarital sex. The dilemma for women is that having sex can cause a loss of face with parents and potential mates and result in remaining single; not having sex means losing face with one's peers. A common solution is "everything but"—engaging in all forms of sex except for vaginal penetration. Anal sex is becoming more widespread and the medical reconstruction of the hymen, although illegal, is becoming more frequent (Mahdavi 2009).

Marriage and Fidelity

Under continuing cultural pressure, most Iranian women still seek marriage, partly for the chance to be recognized and respected as an adult, partly as a way to escape the surveillance of their families and the morality police, and partly to have a safe space to engage in sex. Women do not experience marriage and children as undermining the sexual revolution, though more girls today than in the past say they prefer to remain single. Young women also acknowledge that marriage comes at a cost, including possibly ultimate unhappiness with their partner. Some would like to marry for love, but that can be a long wait, and a single woman over 30 is at a great disadvantage (Bengali and Mostaghim 2016).

Arranged marriages have significantly declined, but marrying a "good" husband is very important, and parents try to suggest people from their own social networks for their children to date, hoping it will lead to marriage. These suggestions are often followed. In addition to looking for sexiness in a woman, a man also wants a woman from his social class, never a class above (Mahdavi 2009:162). As in India, a woman whose class is above that of her husband is viewed as having a source of power over him. Married women openly discuss using sex to get what they want from their husbands (like a new handbag); they also discuss the importance of fidelity and even more often the possibilities of infidelity. Extramarital affairs appear to be common, for both men and women; many women admit they no longer enjoy their husband's company or their sex life. Divorce is risky, however, because marriage still provides economic security and divorce has negative social consequences. Some women take lovers mainly for sex; for others, it may involve deep romantic love, but they acknowledge that "it messes up your life" (Mahdavi 2009:169).

The Iranian government heavily regulates the internet, but young Iranians have found ways around this and frequently use it to arrange for meeting and having sex. Sometimes the internet serves as a form of courtship, where a couple meets on a website, exchanges emails and photos, and then meets face to face; this can turn into a more intimate relationship or even a marriage. Getting to know someone of the opposite sex via the internet is less risky than dating. The internet is also used for anonymous and therefore safe "cybersex," where "hot" sentiments can be exchanged; for men, it is a less embarrassing way to learn about sex. For some married women cybersex is an outlet for sexual frustration and a safer way of deceiving their husband. Young people do want intimacy, and cyberspace provides an outlet that the government cannot breach (Mahdavi 2009:77). But the government polices the internet. For example, in 2014, six young Iranians, including women without their headscarves, were arrested for posting a YouTube video of themselves dancing on a Tehran rooftop to a United States pop song. In an ironic contradiction, however, while a television broadcast featured the Tehran police chief telling young people not to make such videos, the current moderate president, Hassan Rouhani, was giving a speech telling Iranians to embrace the internet (Gladstone 2014).

Maintaining one's vaginal virginity is still important so oral or anal sex, heavy petting fully clothed, or sex between the thighs frequently takes place in venues like cars, parks, abandoned warehouses, the back seats of taxis, or private homes if parents are away. For many young people, the guilt they experience is outweighed by the pleasure.

Sexual interest may be expressed by flashing headlights, or telephone numbers are passed through car windows. When walking on the street, if a man throws down an object, such as a book, and a woman picks it up, she is signaling her interest in having sex with him (Mahdavi 2009:175). Women are asserting their agency both sexually and socially and creating a social movement aimed at changing both the sexual and the sociopolitical climate, which is still repressive compared to Muslim-minority countries.

Summing up cultural differences between Iran and the United States, one girl said, "It's simple, when you [Americans] want to have fun you go out, and when you want to . . . be spiritual you stay in. In Iran, when we want to be spiritual we go out, and when we want to have fun we stay in" (Mahdavi 2009:184). This formerly underground revolution is now going above ground. By disobeying Islamic laws of dress, comportment, modesty, and heterosocial interaction, young people are rejecting the notion of being Islamic subjects, having to submit, for example, to arranged marriages and not meeting their spouses until their formal engagement. As one young girl said, "I used to think I should marry for love but my family is driving me crazy."

Individuals, families, and governments are all affected by changes occurring in Islamic nations. Even in the heartland of Islam in the Arabic Middle East, Islamic rules are becoming more relaxed (Khalaf and Khalaf 2009), while in other Muslim nations, like Malaysia, Turkey, and Afghanistan, they are becoming more strict. Many of the progressive changes are advanced by brave Muslim women activists: daring to drive in Saudi Arabia (al-Sharif 2017); seeking fertility treatments in Lebanon (Inhorn 2007); defying the acceptance of female circumcision (El Saadawi 1980); or speaking out about the failings of Islam (Manji 2003). As these changes spread, governments react in diverse ways in order to retain Islamic culture while incorporating elements of modernity and globalization.

1. What explains the diversity in Islamic nations regarding female modesty, such as wearing the hijab?
2. What role does "romantic love" appear to play in contemporary Iran? Defend your answer with examples from the text.
3. What are some of the most notable things in this chapter that you learned about sex, love, and marriage in the Islamic world?
4. If you had an opportunity to interview a Muslim woman about female modesty, what questions would you ask her? What questions would you ask a man about the same topic? If you are Muslim, what are your opinions about female modesty?

Chapter Seven

Matriarchy and Matriliny
The Minangkabau of Indonesia

The Minangkabau are a rural, rice-growing **matrilineal** ethnic group in Western Sumatra, Indonesia. They are the world's largest matrilineal group, in the world's largest Muslim society, and the sixth largest ethnic group in Indonesia. The traditional Minangkabau kinship system is organized around mothers and their daughters and sons, rather than around fathers and sons, as is more common in Southeast Asia. In traditional Minangkabau culture, called *adat*, women's substantial power derives from their ownership of land, their control of the households, and their central role in extended kinship relations. Minangkabau culture raises interesting questions about matrilineal kinship, **matriarchy**, and Islam, which came to the Minangkabau in the sixteenth century and is now considered central to Minangkabau culture. Indeed, the term adat derives from the Arabic word for custom. The Indonesian government, which designates Islam as the official religion, has also produced changes in Minangkabau culture, particularly in the realm of marriage and kinship.

MARRIAGE

A husband is like ashes on top of a burned stump of a tree, which blow away quickly with the wind.

— Minangkabau proverb (quoted in Sanday 2002)

Marriage is central in Minangkabau culture, and it is obligatory for young girls to marry, contribute to the household, and produce heirs. For younger women, romantic love as the basis of marriage is an important part of their Indonesian identity. The elders who mainly arrange marriages, however, are more interested in a future husband's economic potential. Indeed, any hints of romance between an unmarried couple make adults suspicious that a young man has "bad intentions." Relatives caution a girl's mother to control a rebellious daughter who thinks she is in love. Minangkabau experience suggests that a daughter's romantic interest results in a sexual union and that a boy will break up with the girl he has deflowered. Custom holds that virginity is not to be given to a boyfriend but is to be saved for a husband. Theoretically, if a man finds out on his wedding night that a girl is not a virgin, he can reject her, though in fact this rarely happens. If a girl becomes pregnant prior to marriage, both families make sure the couple gets married.

In the past, Minangkabau girls married very young, often in early adolescence, and older women today generally have been married several times. The parents arrange these first marriages to men much older than the girl, based on his wealth and status. Later in life, a wife often divorces her first husband to marry a man closer to her own age—one whom she chooses herself. As one woman said, "The first husband pays off our debt to our mother; we choose who we want after that" (Sanday 2002:119–120). A woman who chooses a second husband later in life is motivated by both love and the desire to achieve economic security from her husband's income. Distinctions of wealth within the community are always considered in choosing a marriage partner, and a husband's prestige is important in shaping his role in his wife's household.

The age of marriage has greatly increased over the last Minangkabau generation, partly because more girls are furthering their education and working independently outside the home. Young women today say they would never marry an older man chosen by their mother. "If we follow [our parents'] choice, who is happy? If you divorce and are unhappy, that's no good. We have to make ourselves happy first, we can't please our parents" (Blackwood 2000:87). While the appeal of the "romantic" ideal of marriage and a girl's right to find her own husband or even run away to get married is increasing, elder kin are still involved in finding a "good" husband for their female relatives. Senior women today have ceded some ground and are more willing than previously to allow their daughters some leeway in choosing their husbands. Both girls and their mothers value a husband's ability and willingness to help support their kin group, and most girls will not rebel against their family's wishes.

The elaborateness of Minangkabau weddings indicates the importance of marriage in their society, and the ceremonies take place over several weeks. The larger the kin group that attends a wedding, the more status accrues to the family (Sanday 2002:125–127). On her wedding day, a bride, along with her maternal kin, collects her husband from his mother's house and takes him to her mother's house. This is where the couple will live until they establish a household of their own, usually on land owned by the bride's matrilineal clan. Wedding costs are substantial for both parties, and bridewealth and a dowry must be exchanged to cement the marriage.

THE BIG HOUSE

The "big house," identified with the matrilineal family, is the central site of Minangkabau social relations. These structures, among wealthy families, are impressive: they incorporate many house posts, have peaked zinc roofs, and are made of highly decorative wood siding. The big house usually contains an extended family of several generations, including a senior woman, her daughter(s), and their husbands and children. Compartments at one end of the house are for a mother and her daughters, while the front half of the house is an open space for public gatherings and ceremonies. The central house post is identified with the senior woman, who is called "the central pillar of the big house."

The big house is identified with the matrilineal family and structured to accommodate each new marriage. The big house, along with its land, is the most important matrilineal inheritance among the Minangkabau.

When a Minangkabau daughter marries, she and her husband move into her mother's big house. Each newly married daughter resides with her husband at the end compartment farthest from the central house post, and elder married sisters move down the line toward the central post. Sons leave the house at marriage to move in with their wives, but one room next to the kitchen may be designated as the men's room for any divorced or widowed men who return home. Women dominate the big house symbolically and in practice, both in daily life and during elaborate ceremonies. As sons marry out, they no longer participate in ordinary household affairs and only take center stage temporarily during rituals. Many husbands spend much of their time working away from the house and return only in the evenings; some are away for long periods working elsewhere in Indonesia.

In Minangkabau culture, women inherit and control matrilineal property. Once daughters are given land by their mothers after marriage they decide how to use it and control the distribution of its agricultural produce and income. No one can interfere with a senior woman's right to dispose of her land as she wishes. Sons may be given use rights if land is available and their mothers are willing to help them out, but they cannot pass matrilineal land on to their children. Possibly because sons have more opportunities to engage in wage labor, daughters have priority in receiving land.

The kin group of a common ancestress, usually three generations, holds common interest in the land and the big house. This group includes mothers, sisters, and daughters, who live together in the household and share family resources, but the big house may also include just two generations consisting of a mother and a recently married daughter and her husband.

The mother–daughter relationship is the center of big house social life, which persists over generations as daughters are born, marry, bear children, and eventually achieve the position of senior women themselves. Sometimes a younger daughter leaves the big house and establishes her own house, often very near her mother's, on their matrilineal land. In some big houses, mother and daughters share the produce of their undivided rice fields, but daughters also have access to additional income, either from their husbands or from small-scale businesses they run themselves. This income can give them some highly desired independence from their mother's control.

In elite families, the main income derives from the rice land belonging to the big house, all of which ultimately will belong to the daughters. Senior women use the income from the rice land to pay for common household needs. This sharing of resources illustrates the mutual cooperation and assistance among kin, which is a traditional Minangkabau cultural value. Although household and farm tasks are separated by gender, everyone is expected to help out, and all big house members provide some form of unpaid labor or contribute cash to the household.

GENDER ROLES

Child care arrangements are flexible; a married daughter may stay at home while her mother works, or she may work while her mother cares for her children. Preteen boys and girls watch younger siblings; mothers leave small children with various adults; in addition to watching their siblings, young girls help their mothers clean the house while boys tend to the small animals. Unmarried daughters weed the rice fields, and adult married daughters plant, weed, and harvest rice on the family land. Usually, the eldest daughter eventually takes over as the senior woman. Unmarried sons help by carrying sacks of unhusked rice to be milled. This traditional expectation of cooperation is buttressed by the traditional Asian respect for elders. This means that younger family members generally defer to the needs and decisions of the older generation, while senior women see their primary responsibility as guiding their children into responsible adulthood (Blackwood 2000:61).

As senior women become elderly, household management falls more to their daughters, as does the work and supervision of the rice fields. But all family members support the big house through joint efforts based on consultation, consensus, and cooperation. Big house group efforts also reflect the Minangkabau belief that women are productive individuals and that whoever brings money into the household has the right to control its disposal. A rural Minangkabau woman expects to earn or produce her own income but also expects and depends on resources and assistance from other family members. This includes her husband, who, if he contributes support, is regarded as an "honored guest" in the house.

A married son maintains a strong interest in his mother's kin group, for whom he has specific responsibilities and obligations, particularly regarding ceremonial participation. As sons or brothers, the relation of men with their maternal kin depends mainly on age and rank. Mothers provide strong emotional support to their sons throughout their lives, and a son must cooperate with his mother in return. A mother who is displeased with her son may take back the rice land she has given him, or refuse to allow him to return home after a divorce, even though it is his right. The many young unmarried men who work outside the village usually send home some of their wages to their mothers. These obligations of a son to his mother and other kinswomen last throughout his lifetime. He may work on, or occasionally supervise, his mother's rice fields to increase production, or buy new land for her. A married son remains part of the family with an equal voice and even has substantial influence in family matters if he proves himself a reliable source of family support. Men who carry the family title have more weight in family decision-making, especially regarding marriages of their female kin. But even titled men must prove their competence in managing family affairs before they are given much control.

Basically, however, a man is a marginal member of the big house of both his own and his wife's family and only periodically interacts with his kinswomen. In the past, a son-in-law was a temporary resident in his wife's family house, visiting at night and returning to his mother's house in the morning. This has changed somewhat, and a resident husband is now expected to provide additional labor, land, or income to the household. Yet he does not participate in decision-making in his wife's family affairs although he may voice an opinion in ceremonial deliberations and offer help out of respect for his wife's family.

While in the past, husbands only occasionally gave money to their wives for child care, today there is an increasing expectation that they will take on more financial responsibility. This is partly due to the Indonesian government's emphasis on the patriarchal nuclear family and its accompanying requirement about a woman's rights to her husband's income. A husband decides on the disposal of his income but is influenced by the expectations of his wife's family.

In general, husbands are considered unreliable and irresponsible, and wives may complain to the senior women of their husband's family if he fails to contribute his fair share to the household. An elite man may ask for a percentage of his mother's rice land, and a generous mother will help out an industrious son; the income from the land is then split between his wife's and his mother's big house.

CONFLICTS IN MARRIAGE

The dual expectations that a man must provide material assistance to his own and to his wife's family often puts Minangkabau men in a difficult position, creating tension between a man's role as a husband and as a son. If men are farmers, they may provide uncompensated labor in the big house rice fields or supplement the household income through agricultural or wage labor. There are no set rules for dividing a man's income between his wife's family and his own mother's house. Indonesia's current emphasis puts the interests of the nuclear family before that of a man's own matrilineal kin, which runs counter to Minangkabau tradition but is being integrated into their culture.

The current Indonesian emphasis on the nuclear family allows husbands and fathers to maintain enduring ties with their children even after divorce or remarriage. Yet, while a husband is valued for his reproductive capabilities and his economic support for his wife's big house, he has little power in his household. A man who does not show respect to senior women or help support his wife's kin creates tension in his marriage and his household.

In spite of the traditionally close ties between mothers and daughters, this relationship, too, can be filled with tension. While a daughter's marriage to a wealthy or high-status man contributes to the prestige of her kin group, she also feels forced to follow her mother's will, especially since disagreement can affect her inheritance of land. Nevertheless, a daughter has choices: she can stay home after her marriage and follow her mother's will, build her own house, or leave the village to look for other opportunities. Marriage is central to this decision.

All Minangkabau are expected, encouraged, or even forced to marry, and single people are not considered adults. As in many cultures, the imperative for marriage goes beyond the requirement to reproduce; marriage also constructs an extended network of kin that is the basis of village social life. For the Minangkabau woman, continuation and expansion of the matrilineal kinship network through marriage and children are critical to her own standing in the kin group and in the community. An unmarried or childless daughter loses respect and influence in these social networks. Thus, senior women are invested in controlling young women, both to avoid a bad marriage or to make sure they get married (Blackwood 2000:77).

ISLAM, THE INDONESIAN STATE, AND CULTURAL CHANGE

What we know about Minangkabau matriliny comes from their ancestors, government officials, the local middle class and anthropologists.

— Blackwood (2000)

Twenty years after the Indonesian nation was created in 1945, a New Order government emerged that aimed at creating a "modern" state, which fostered economic development and Indonesian unity, and declared Sunni Islam as the state religion. Rural ethnic groups were viewed as backward farmers, and many Minangkabau practices and beliefs, such as matriliny, the importance of the extended matrifocal family, the power of women, and non-Islamic weddings, were viewed as obstacles to the new ideology. Today, the Indonesian government no longer recognizes Minangkabau marriages that are conducted in a religion other than Islam, and as described below, the Minangkabau are trying to adapt in a variety of ways to these changes.

The "masculinist" cultures of Dutch colonialism, modern Islam, industrialization and agricultural development, official state ideology, and state-supported popular media all denigrated matrilineality and the extensive powers of women in Minangkabau culture. In contrast to Minangkabau commitment to their traditional kinship and gender system, Indonesia's contemporary national culture views the nuclear family as the most important kin group and sees women's role as dependent caretakers of home, husband, and children. The government promotes this female identity through political propaganda and through its schools, which disparage the values of rural life and matrilineal kinship. It organizes mandatory women's groups to further the national ideology and Islam, which discourages Minangkabau practices as contrary to the Qur'an (Blackwood 2000:30–31). Both men and women are encouraged to find work as a way out of the village and as a means to a higher status and salaried jobs.

Islamic gender ideology does not contain powerful roles for women but does provide new sources of authority for men. For example, unlike men, women are not permitted to have an authoritative role in public ritual occasions or to become Islamic leaders (Mazumdar and Mazumdar 1999). Government financing of village projects also supports Islam, as in the upgrading and construction of modern prayer houses. The end of Ramadan is celebrated in village-wide prayer ceremonies, which most people attend. Speeches and prayers urge the villagers to apply the wisdom of Islam to their daily lives (Blackwood 2000:86).

The Indonesian government encourages a modern Islamic feminine identity in many ways. It organizes classes for the wives of government officials in cooking, etiquette, sewing, flower arrangement, family planning, health, and nutrition, and it hosts events promoting Western beauty products and fashions. This modern feminine identity is supported by media advertisements for cosmetics, clothing, and accessories that contribute to the image of the dependent housewife as central to marital happiness and a good, urban, middle-class life. Women are bombarded with magazines and television shows that promote a national dress code including jewelry and makeup and skirts and dresses as the only acceptable attire for work. Professional occupations are encouraged as long as women put their families first. This entails being a good housewife and mother whose main responsibilities are for the well-being of the household; it is the man who is viewed as the household head. This ideology appears to be widely accepted by younger Minangkabau women as well as men (Blackwood 2000:83, 89).

The Indonesian state makes room for traditional Minangkabau rituals as part of their goal to retain Minangkabau allegiance to Islam.

The efforts of the government, as well as the Islamic hierarchy, have had a great effect on the Minangkabau, and matriliny, matriarchy, and Islam are now all central to Minangkabau culture and identity. Indeed, the word of Islam is an inseparable part of Minangkabau ideology, which is defined as *Adat Islamiah*, that is, adat in accordance with Islamic principles. Incorporating this ideology into daily life and practice is not easy: adat law, Islamic law, and Indonesian national law contradict each other in many ways, particularly regarding gender roles, the ownership of property, inheritance rules, and marriage patterns (Elfira 2009; Blackwood 2000:17–19). For example, in 1953, representatives of the Minangkabau, along with those of the Indonesian government, declared that while ancestral property would still be inherited according to matrilineal principles, self-acquired property would be inherited based on Sharia law, under which sons would inherit twice as much as daughters. And in 1976, the Indonesian Supreme Court held that "family" refers to the nuclear family and that the father is considered the family head (Elfira 2009). The Indonesian government uses various kinds of public media, such as billboards, to reinforce the Islamic component of Minangkabau adat.

One factor currently affecting marriage among the Minangkabau is the increasing influence of Christianization, which many Minangkabau fear is undermining their culture. One of the ways Christianity penetrates Minangkabau culture is through intermarriage, defined as marriage between a Muslim and a non-Muslim. While previously, intermarriage was permitted through registration with the Civil Registry Office, in 1983, the government narrowed this permission to apply only if the marriage did not involve a Muslim. Still, some opportunities for Muslim–non-Muslim intermarriage remain; one option is to perform the marriage overseas and then register it officially in the Civil Registry. Because this can be expensive, some couples choose the option to undergo a formal ceremony according to the rites of one of the spouse's religion; this, however, requires the other spouse to leave his or her former religion. In this case, the marriage rite is often a formality; in practice, the person who converts does so in a formal sense only and actually retains his or her religion in practice and as part of his or her identity. This form of marriage is preferred by low- and lower middle-class Minangkabau (Elfira 2009).

Islam permits a Muslim man to marry a non-Muslim woman as long as the marriage is performed according to Muslim law—but not the reverse. Minangkabau society is also more tolerant of this kind of marriage, reflecting the Islamic value that a man's function is as the head of his family and the guardian of his wife. If the man is Christian, there is a fear that he will persuade or "force" his wife to follow his religion and abandon her own. The Minangkabau are still committed to both matriliny and the importance of women in their society; they view women as more active defenders of traditional Minangkabau culture and fear that intermarriage may result in Minangkabau "becom[ing] a Christian land," and the end of the Minangkabau. To prevent this possibility, the Minangkabau deprive women who intermarry of their inheritance, forbid their rise to senior matrilineal leadership, and exclude them from adat gatherings (Elfira 2009:176).

TRADITIONAL MATRIARCHY: WILL IT CONTINUE?

While many anthropologists consider the mother's brother rather than the mother as central in Minangkabau society, Evelyn Blackwood (2000) and Peggy Sanday (2002) persuasively challenge this theory. They claim that this perspective reflects a bias in Western anthropology that ignored the significant formal and informal power wielded by senior Minangkabau women. Blackwood and Sanday, among others, point out, that even today, women have the right as lineage elders to control ancestral land, decisively intervene in discussions on ceremonial practices, and control subordinate kin. Even today, as daughters leave the village for schooling and work, they maintain a lifelong connection to their home guided by matrilineal principles (Blackwood 2000:3).

Male power mainly includes recognition of a brother's right to protect the big house of his birth, to protect the matrilineally owned land, and to take responsibility for his sister's children above his own. A man's lack of importance in his wife's big house is balanced by his importance in his own natal house. Men are important as brothers and sons, but peripheral as husbands, although as noted above, this is changing.

In spite of the declaration in the Indonesian constitution that all Indonesian citizens are considered equal, the contemporary government ideology aims at replacing the power of the extended matrilineal family and Minangkabau identity with a national emphasis on a male-dominated nuclear family, higher education, wealth, social mobility, economic development, and modernity. While Islam and government policies and practices have affected Minangkabau matrilineality, anthropologists Blackwood (2000) and Sanday (2002) stress that the central value of Minangkabau village life still revolves around the matrilineage, which is not disappearing but is being reshaped, and that women retain considerable power. The Minangkabau have been somewhat successful in sustaining Minangkabau identity and a culture that integrates adat, Islam, and Indonesian ideology, but not without some tension and anxiety and continuous subtle and informal negotiations regarding marriage and family relations.

1. Describe some of the bases of men and women's power in Minangkabau culture. How are these changing in contemporary Indonesia?
2. Do you think the Indonesian government is justified in attempting to replace Minangkabau matriliny with the male-dominated nuclear family? Why or why not?
3. Given the goals of the contemporary Indonesian state, do you think romantic love can become the dominant basis of Minangkabau marriages? Explain your reasons.
4. Do you think the powerful position of women in Minangkabau society will continue? Why or Why not?

Chapter Eight

Courtship, Marriage, and Fidelity

The Igbo of Nigeria

There is no romance without finance.

— Smith (2009b)

This chapter examines changes in courtship, sexuality, romance, and marriage among the Igbo, an ethnic group in southeastern Nigeria, known throughout Africa for their entrepreneurial skill, their receptivity to change, and their willingness to migrate both within Nigeria and abroad, in order to pursue their economic interests (Smith 2009a:90).

In Western academic descriptions of Africa, the concept of love has been greatly overshadowed by the study of kinship and marriage (Cole and Thomas 2009). Romantic love in Africa, while occasionally noted in the past, has never been the basis of marriage. This is rapidly changing, however, due to modernization, globalization, the incursion of modern media such as the internet and cell phones, the rise of urban migration, and the growing number of Africans receiving a higher education. These changes take diverse forms throughout Africa, depending on the indigenous culture, political history, and the impact of Islam and Christianity, but clearly a Westernized concept of love as a basis for marriage is spreading widely around the continent.

Patriarchy, patrilocality, patriliny, and polygyny, the marriage of one man to more than one woman, are all important common cultural elements in African societies, including the Igbo. The social pressures of Western and Christian condemnation of polygyny, as well as the fact that few men can afford more than one wife, have led to its decline in some parts of Africa (Kilbride 2006), including West Africa. The demise of polygyny appears to be exaggerated, however, and it is perhaps more accurate to say that it is adapting to global and local changes, particularly in Nigerian cities. Contemporary polygyny has also been affected by modern notions of romantic love and companionate marriage, the tendency of marriage unions to become more informal and fragile (due partly to periods of economic crisis and partly to the diminishing control by elders over the lives of young people), the rising age at which people get married, and the increasing importance of free choice of spouses (Whitehouse 2018), as described below.

Patrilocality has also declined, especially among the Igbo, due to urban migration, though patriarchy is alive and well. It takes different forms than in the past, however, and is somewhat undermined, at least on the surface, by the ideology of conjugal love. The exchange of goods and services between the bride's family and the groom's family, which seals and stabilizes a marriage, is a widespread African tradition and remains central to Igbo marriages.

The Igbo are also patrilineal, and a person must marry outside his or her patrilineage, as marriages traditionally create important alliances with nearby communities. Marriages were mostly arranged by elder kin; occasionally young men and women would defy family demands, although this often resulted in unhappiness for the married couple. Today, with the increasing value of individualism, kin groups are losing direct control over their children's choice of spouses, although they remain important both in indirectly arranging marriages and even more so in keeping marriages stable.

COURTSHIP AND MARRIAGE

With or without an expectation of marriage, urban courtship among the Igbo is based on a culture of pleasure and consumerism: gift exchange, eating out in expensive restaurants, dancing in discos, and often, premarital sex. Men are primarily attracted to a woman's beauty, and for women, the main attraction is the man's ability to display and offer symbols of wealth, such as a car and a willingness to support the couple's pleasurable activities. Both courtship and marriage put extra pressures on men to participate in elite or middle-class consumption, such as acquiring cell phones, TVs, DVD players, and fashionable clothes even as their economic positions become more precarious in contemporary Nigeria (Smith 2009a).

Courtship, marriage, fatherhood, and pre- and extramarital relationships are expensive, and a man's ability to sustain these expenses is an important aspect of his masculinity. Igbo masculinity is highly valued, and its display in public and in intimate relationships is essential for Igbo men. The rise of romantic love has exacerbated this cultural pattern and has affected men's behavior. As anthropologist Daniel Smith notes, "Men must now win women's hearts as well as raise the money for bridewealth" (2017:60). Men also take a greater role in child care that previously fell on their wives and their extended families. The great amount of money needed for displaying masculinity, in all social classes, is difficult to acquire in Nigeria's unstable economy. Providing proper and elaborate burials for their fathers, as well as lavish weddings for their children, are central occasions for public displays of masculinity. One result of these many pressures is an increase in crime and violence, including domestic violence, as men become more insecure about their ability to demonstrate their masculinity (Smith 2017).

The sophisticated urban Igbo man flaunts luxury items such as dapper versions of traditional dress and sociability as part of his masculine image.

> *A lot of things are important in deciding whom to marry. You need a good husband who can provide for the family and it's important to find a man who is progressive. I would never marry a man who just wanted his wife to cater to him like a servant.*
>
> — quoted in Smith (2006)

Contemporary Igbo have ideologically embraced romantic love as the basis of mate selection and marriage and as a key factor in the personal relationship of the married couple (Smith 2009a). The popularity of romance as the basis for marriage first appeared in Nigerian popular literature just after World War II, and today most young Igbo choose their own spouses; among educated youth, this is nearly universal (Smith 2001:131). Yet, the support and approval of the kin group remain critical for marriages to succeed. Once a couple is married, the main interest of their kin is fertility, and successful parenthood is still considered the defining attribute of full personhood in Igbo culture.

The contrasting values placed on love and fertility highlights the dramatic differences between courtship and marriage. Courtship privileges a couple's personal relationship negotiated through interpersonal intimacy and expressions of love. Marriage, in contrast, is constructed within the framework of continuing ties and obligations to the extended family and community and privileges the social roles of mother and father. This pattern affects gender roles: while modern courtship supports an egalitarian gender dynamic, marriage continues to uphold the gender inequality of patriarchy, with husbands having more power and authority than wives.

Urban migration is central in the changing patterns of both courtship and marriage. In cities, women especially are less subject to the surveillance and regulation of their kin, and urban living gives young people a chance to meet many other Nigerians with whom they can socialize, develop romantic relationships, and engage in sex. During courtship both partners feel obliged to be faithful, although this is not always observed; if an unfaithful partner is caught, the other person will probably end the relationship. Men cheat more than women, but the issue is considered merely personal and of little interest to anyone besides the couple involved.

A woman's premarital experiences prepare her for negotiations over love, money, and fidelity, which are different in marriage, and although women marry for love, it is not only for love. They expect their husbands to be good providers, responsible fathers, and socially responsible men who present a positive public view of the marriage. These concerns underlie women's responses to infidelity.

The Igbo today highly value choosing one's mate and the importance of the personal and emotional quality of the conjugal relationship; this is the concept of "modern" love (Smith 2009a:161). This view is almost universal among young, more highly educated, and urban Igbo, both men and women, although it is also gaining ground in rural areas and among those of lower status.

> *One young woman, comparing her own marriage to that of her parents said, "My father had three wives and fourteen children. Often it was every woman for herself. My husband and I have a partnership. We decide things. There is love between us."*
>
> — Smith (2001:137)

In spite of many changes in Igbo marriage, patrilocality, patriarchy and patriliny, remain strong, as does the emphasis on fertility and parenthood as a source of a person's most highly valued social identity. One traditional aspect of Igbo marriage that has remained unchanged is the exclusion of marriage partners from non-Igbo ethnic groups. Also completely excluded as spouses are individuals from the former Igbo slave class (*osu*), even though slavery is outlawed in Nigeria and discriminating against the osu is condemned by Christianity, the major Igbo religion (Smith 2001:137).

Igbo marry in both traditional and Christian, or "white," ceremonies; very often in both. The traditional ceremony is obligatory (and much more costly); if it is not performed the couple is not married in the eyes of their kin and the wider community. A marriage is legitimatized through the exchange of obligations and rights. The transfer of a woman's reproductive capacity from her patrilineage to her husband's through the payment of bridewealth establishes an enduring social alliance and a lifetime series of exchanges of rights and obligations between the bride and the groom's kin. Central to this alliance is the mutual interest in the children produced by the marriage; prayers ask God to grant the couple many offspring. The traditional ceremony emphasizes traditional Igbo values about extended families; most guests wear traditional clothing, as does the marital couple, and the speeches and festivities of dance and music reflect traditional Igbo styles. Elders urge the couple to be mindful of their obligations to their own and their **affinal kin**, and the guests attending the ceremony are reminded to give support to the couple when needed.

The Christian ceremony is more a symbol of upward mobility and progressiveness; the wedding practices are distinctly Western: the bride wears a white wedding dress, the festivities include a ceremonial cutting of a wedding cake, but most importantly, the minister or priest emphasizes that the success of the marriage depends on the individual couple and their relationship with each other, reinforcing a Western companionate model of marriage.

Couples today are far more likely to share a bedroom, eat together, maintain a single household budget, and live in a town or city away from the family compound. But once the couple is married, the importance of their personal relationship as a reflection of the state of the marriage is replaced by the emphasis on successful parenthood. In addition to having and caring for children as a means to individual personhood, fulfilling one's obligations to the community is also essential. At the same time, fertility is an area in which the couple can exercise choices with regard to when to have children and how many to have. About a third of young Igbo couples use family planning methods (Smith 2001:140). Igbo men who cannot father a biological child may look the other way to enable their wives to get pregnant by another man; socially recognized fatherhood is always ascribed to the man who paid the bridewealth for the woman.

Divorce is almost totally socially unacceptable among the Igbo and occurs mainly in the case of infertile couples. Deteriorating personal issues between the husband and wife are not considered an acceptable reason for divorce. If a wife complains that her husband fails to support his children, she has much more leverage than if she complains of personal problems. Threats of divorce always bring in extended family members on both sides, who see it as their responsibility to find a way to bring the couple back together.

ENABLING MALE INFIDELITY

Despite the verbal commitment to modern marriage, which ideally implies gender equality, the different standards of marital fidelity for men and women are based on unequal male privilege and power. The far greater occurrence of male infidelity is enabled by several factors (Smith 2009b:166). Work-related urban migration takes Igbo men away from their wives and families and provides the opportunities for extramarital relationships; men frequently attribute their infidelity to the opportunities and hardship produced by these absences. In addition, extramarital relationships resulting from work-related migration can be more easily hidden from wives, family, and neighbors and are relatively anonymous.

On the other hand, close ties and obligations of kinship and the rural community remain strong, although often experienced by men as an economic and social burden. Traditional Igbo marriages between individuals from neighboring villages permitted affinal kin to make alliances both in the interest of intercommunity peace and trade. These relationships remain important for access to the resources of the Nigerian economy today. In addition, if a husband in this patrilocal society is from a far away village, the wife's family cannot easily monitor the marriage and will not be involved in the lives of the children, who may become important economic resources. Thus, families try to discourage these marriages. Although there may also be advantages in having wider geographical networks, most people still marry close to home (Smith 2001).

Another important factor enabling male infidelity is the pervasiveness of all-male peer groups, which are a modern form of the traditional Igbo sex-segregated social organization. Even more than in most societies, all-male social groups dominate the lives of Igbo men. Male-dominated urban spaces for sociability, such as bars, social clubs, and sports clubs, reinforce male peer group dynamics that reward men for their presentation of high economic status and masculine sexuality

(Smith 2017). In these places, where they meet up with their girlfriends, there is little expectation that they will encounter their wives or their wives' friends or relatives. Even when men do not display their lovers in social clubs, their affairs are a central topic of conversation, and most men want their peers to know about their extramarital affairs. Thus, these public spaces allow the interweaving of the many dimensions of the prestige of extramarital relations: masculinity, virility, consumption, and social class, along with sex. A man's girlfriends also know the rules about relations with their married partners, such as never showing up at a man's house or publically accosting him or his wife, and they also benefit economically by obeying the rules. If they get pregnant, they have abortions, which are illegal, but widespread, and indeed dangerous (Smith 2009b). It is widely accepted that an Igbo man can and will have extramarital affairs, and there is a certain pride in taking lovers. As long as he continues to provide for his wife and children, there is little social condemnation.

Having many extramarital partners is a mark of economic status as well as virility. The man who has a car, belongs to a social club, rents expensive hotel rooms, and gives his girlfriends expensive gifts and substantial cash is widely desired by women. These elite men are called "sugar daddies"; the young women, often seeking higher education or employed in an urban office or business, wear makeup, straighten their hair, wear fashionable clothes, and see school and the city as a means to a better life. They routinely ask for money to pay school fees, start a business, help their parents, help pay rent, and buy clothes, jewelry, and even electronics and appliances, though they avoid asking for this assistance as a payment for sex. Men commonly refer to these women as "handbags," indicating the men are in charge of the relationship (Smith 2001:142); when men travel to neighboring towns or cities, their friends often ask them if they are "carrying a handbag" (Smith 2006:148). The relationship between these married men and their lovers poses a contradiction: the men say they are not swayed by these women, but many believe that women can gain power over them through love medicine. So, the paradox: these women are clearly used by men, but also clearly use men.

Although a wife has little control over her husband's extramarital affairs, there are rules men must follow: never confront their wives with their infidelity, never jeopardize the family's well-being by spending too much time or money on a lover, and never let the lover break up the marriage. A lover can phone a man at work, but never at the man's home; the sexual liaisons take place in hotels, never in the man's house; and the lover never challenges a wife in a stare down; nor do these lovers expect the man to leave his wife to marry them, and they know not to get pregnant.

INFIDELITY AND GENDER ROLES

An Igbo wife wants and, perhaps in spite of the widespread knowledge to the contrary, expects her husband to be faithful. She tries to assure this by manipulating her husband's affection and reminding him of the Christian concept of monogamy. A wife who works can use her control over some of the economic resources as leverage in getting her husband to behave. But even among professional women, it is the role of wife and mother that is highly valued, and a woman's status is still not equal to a man's. Although gossip spreads that a woman may also be having an extramarital affair, the main battle is between a husband who wants and thinks he is entitled to his wife's fidelity and a wife who wants to rein in her husband's infidelity. The wider kin and community group is also much less sympathetic and more willing to chastise a woman's infidelity than a man's.

In traditional Igbo society female chastity before marriage was highly valued and made easier by the very young age at which girls married. In 1960 the average marriage age for girls was 16, and it is now 21; many women remain single until their late twenties. Men also marry later—around the age of 30—when they are more economically secure and can afford bridewealth and support a family. In addition, with more single young people in Nigeria's cities, they are more exposed to peer and media messages about the appeal and acceptability of premarital sex. Premarital sexuality is also more acceptable because sexual identities and commodity consumption have become significant aspects of contemporary courtship (Smith 2006:140–141). Furthermore, because courtship plays no real role in reproduction, love and sexuality can be—and are—regarded with little interest by the larger community before marriage. Once married, however, the personal lives of the couple become community property. In this patrilineal society, a woman who challenges her husband's infidelity, cheats on her husband, or breaks up the marriage risks losing her children both for herself and for her lineage. This explains the difference in attitudes toward premarital sex and marital infidelity.

While it appears that Igbo men are as committed as women to an ideology of marriage based on love, men also rationalize their extramarital sexuality by referring to the Igbo traditional patriarchal pattern, which gives men this entitlement. And even though the economy has changed from agriculture, where land ownership was highly significant, to an urban economy with the growth of wage labor and government jobs, the need for helpful networks and the utility of children's support continue to maintain the traditional value of kinship and community ties. Thus, while globalization, modernization,

In spite of the independence and professional success of many Igbo women, fertility remains an essential aspect of female adult identity. Parenthood makes it difficult for married women to have leverage over their husband's fidelity.

urban migration, education, and widely circulating ideas about love would seem to provide women with equality in sexuality and mate selection, married women remain subject to traditional patriarchal values. Because of the importance of parenthood and the continuing need for kinship ties in securing social resources, marriage based on love has not much improved women's status in relation to men.

THE RISKS OF HIV

Finally, and perhaps most tragically, the increase in love marriages and individual choice in selecting marriage partners, and the multiple extramarital sexual relationships of men, have complicated decisions on the use of condoms and place many women at risk for contracting HIV from their partners (Hirsch and Wardlow 2006; Hirsch et al. 2009). This is true not just for the Igbo and calls attention to the relationship of culture to the spread of AIDS throughout Africa (Feldman 2008). Among the Igbo, the patterns and expectations about gender roles established in courtship create difficulties for women in trying to negotiate safe sex after marriage, where the roles of wife and mother are paramount. Indeed, among educated young people, there is disagreement about whether decisions about contraception are a man's responsibility, a woman's responsibility, or a joint responsibility. Prior to the awareness of the AIDS epidemic, these discussions mainly concerned unwanted pregnancies. Now, with the awareness of the sexual transmission of HIV, and the protection afforded by condom use, a woman who suggests this to her husband implies that either she or he is unsafe to have sex with. It is also believed that condoms inhibit intimacy and pleasure, and, more importantly, most young Nigerians still associate AIDS with immoral sexuality or gay male sexual orientation.

The ideals of monogamy and companionate love in the context of continuing gender inequality combined with the continued importance of fertility inhibit a woman's ability to negotiate condom use, even when she knows or suspects her husband is unfaithful (Smith 2006:143). And while more women are now employed outside the home, this has not really changed the dynamics of power in the household. As ethnography in a wide range of cultures, including the Igbo, indicates, love marriages, rather than protecting women, contribute to the risk of women contracting HIV from their unfaithful husbands.

1. Describe three highly significant roles that money currently plays in Igbo relationships.
2. What is the current role of kinship among the Igbo and how is this both similar to and different from how it was in the past?
3. Describe some of the aspects of Igbo culture and social organization that enable male infidelity.
4. How is the spread of HIV related to the importance of love as the basis of Igbo marriage?

Chapter Nine

Fact and Fantasy
Sexuality in Polynesia

What we see depends mainly on what we look for.

— John Lubbock (*The Beauties of Nature and the Wonders of the World We Live In*)

European explorers first reached Samoa in the early eighteenth century and were awed by what they found, describing it as a world untouched by civilization, where people lived in harmony with nature and embraced a culture of unrestricted sexuality. The stories of European explorations caused a sensation in the West, fueling romantic fantasies (Kirk 2012). In 1830, Protestant missionaries arrived in Samoa and were largely successful in converting the Samoans to Christianity, although the Samoans did not altogether abandon their traditional culture and religious beliefs.

The missionaries' perception of Samoan culture focused mainly on sexuality and family structure. They were shocked by many traditional Samoan practices, such as polygyny, extramarital intercourse, easy divorce, the performance of "lewd" songs and dances, the public testing of virginity at marriage, tattooing, wearing revealing clothing, and the lack of privacy in Samoan houses. In short, the missionaries viewed Samoa as a pagan culture filled with godlessness and immorality and in need of substantial reform (Shankman 1996:558).

Western contact in the nineteenth, twentieth, and twenty-first centuries brought many changes to Samoa. Historians and anthropologists disagree about the elements of "traditional" Samoan culture, which contained many contradictions and ambiguities largely overlooked in early descriptions (Shore 1981:197). Western colonialism significantly reshaped economies and governments throughout Polynesia, and today American Samoa is a United States territory. In this chapter, I first describe traditional Polynesian culture, including that of Samoa, and then describe some significant changes and current issues of debate.

HIERARCHY AND KINSHIP

Indigenous Polynesian societies were mainly **chiefdoms**, independent political units incorporating multiple villages under the permanent control of a paramount chief (Carneiro 1981:45). The chiefly office was inherited within the family and supported by *mana,* a spiritual power that was both innate and inherited. Polynesian chiefdoms were based on highly productive horticultural economies resulting in a surplus of food, which was controlled and redistributed by the chief throughout the society. In the Polynesian ranking system, chiefly families were at the top, followed by high-ranking lineages just below them and a commoner population at the bottom. Prestige and rank were central to patterns of gender, sexuality, and marriage, which created important distinctions between women as wives, mothers, or sisters (Ortner 1981; Shore 1981).

From the perspective of the Western missionaries, eroticism and sexual activity were excessive in Polynesian culture. Women played an essential role in their societies; relations between men and women were relatively harmonious, but it was hardly the "paradise of liberation" fantasized by the West. Sexuality was also not as free as the missionaries perceived and was actually subject to surveillance and strict rules. A major goal of Polynesian culture was the enhancement of one's personal prestige and status, achieved mainly through manipulation of the rules of descent, marriage, and residence. Descent groups linked by blood (**lineages**) were the major kinship units, and ranking within lineages was based on the birth order of brothers. The oldest brother was senior to the younger brothers, and all the elder brother's descendants were socially superior to descendants of younger brothers. The preferred form of marriage was between **cross cousins** within the same rank, although women frequently married up and men married down. Generally, a person inherited the rank of his or her own father, rather than his or her mother (Ortner 1981:365).

Succession to high office passed through males, but descent group membership passed through both males and females. Adoption within kin groups was common, and a woman who moved to her husband's home often sent one or more of her children to live with her own immediate kin. Ideally, a wife resided with her husband's kin, but daughters could inherit land, so a junior son, or one with little property, might choose to live with his wife's family. Children could also affiliate with their mother's rather than their father's line, which added to the size and status of the wife's lineage. A chief might seek a husband for his daughter who would live in her kin group, thus retaining her children for his lineage. Occasionally chiefs arranged for their daughters to marry into another chief's lineage or even into a lower status group to increase his political dominance (Ortner 1981:367).

SEXUALITY AND VIRGINITY

Few ethnographic topics have caused as much debate as sexuality in the Pacific Islands, particularly Samoa, which along with Tonga, is the original homeland of a distinctive Polynesian culture (Feinberg and Macphersen 2002:126). The perception of the Pacific Islands, and particularly Samoa, as a sexual paradise gained worldwide attention in the 1920s, partly due to the ethnography of Margaret Mead, *Coming of Age in Samoa: A Psychological Study of Primitive Youth for Western Civilization*, which, as Mead herself said, became "a small bombshell." Mead's fieldwork, carried out in 1923, focused on the sex

This painting, *The Day of the God*, painted by Paul Gauguin in 1894, clearly expresses the European fantasies of the South Pacific.

life of adolescent girls, which she described as easy and open, contrasting it to the restrictions and prudery of US adolescents.

The Samoan attitude toward sexuality is complex and was neither as repressed as that of Christian missionaries nor as casual as that in other parts of Polynesia, such as Tahiti. Enforcing the virginity of unmarried girls was central to Samoan culture, although as one missionary noted in the late 1880s, this was more an ideal than a reality (Shankman 1996:559). There are few polite Samoan terms for sexuality, which is associated with aggressive, private impulses. Sexual activities are referred to as play, wrestling, fighting, or "doing bad things" and are clearly distinguished from *aloha,* meaning affectionate love, defined as empathy or respect (Shore 1981:196). In Samoan culture, a girl's virginity was highly prized and controlled by her father and brothers, while the sexual activity of boys was unsupervised and even encouraged.

The most culturally elaborated form of the sexually controlled daughter/sister was the *taupo*, a position of ritual responsibility and honor (Mead 1973/1928:42; Shankman 1996:559; Shore 1981:197). The taupo was most often the chief's daughter; she ranked above the chief's male heir and successor and was even more respected than the chief's wife. Symbolically a daughter/sister to the whole village, the taupo was under strict sexual control and was required to retain her virginity until marriage. Her seduction was considered a public crime and her seducer would be punished by drowning or being beaten to death. A taupo's marriage was publically consummated to prove her virginity, as described below in a late nineteenth-century European account:

> When the guests . . . assembled at the . . . wedding feast, the bride was led in and paraded, naked and trembling. She was seated in the center of the square and the Chief approached, silently seating himself close to and directly facing her. . . . Placing his left hand on her right shoulder, he inserted the two forefingers of his right hand into her vulva. He then held up his arm as the tribe watched eagerly for the drops of blood to trickle down—the sight of which proclaimed the honor of the tribe, the dignity of the chief and the virtue of the bride. (quoted in Danielsson 1956:382)

Proof of a taupo's virginity could be confirmed by publically displaying a bloodstained mat after the marriage consummation. A taupo whose virginity was not confirmed was beaten by her female relatives (Ortner 1981:372). The taupo's virginity symbolized the effective control of her male kinsmen. While ensuring a girl's virginity was necessary to build the status of the lineage in all ranks, unmarried boys were encouraged to be as sexually active as possible and their sexuality was associated with vitality and political power (Shore 1981:200). Although premarital sex was widespread, it was defined as "stolen" from a girl's father and brothers, who had failed to control it. The idea of "stealing sex" explains many Samoan sexual practices such as "sleep crawling," the consuming interest in deflowering virgins, institutionalized elopement, marriage by capture, and displays of hymeneal blood at weddings.

Sleep crawling, which entailed stealthily and unexpectedly entering a girl's house at night and having intercourse with her, was viewed as a sign of masculinity. A boy preferred "sweet talk" to overcome a girl's resistance, as using force could wake up her family, who lived in the same house or even slept in a common room. A Samoan man who was caught and branded as a sleep crawler was considered shameful, and no girl would ever take him seriously (Mead 1930:62).

The preference for virgin wives in Polynesia conflicted with the widespread practice of deflowering virgins, a topic of endless bragging among adolescent boys (Mead 1930:95–96). Elopement and marriage by capture also carried the message of stealing a girl from her father and brothers; if the girl was a taupo from a neighboring village, it was considered a particularly great achievement (Mead 1930:95). The prevalence of rape in Samoa, and Polynesia generally, whether ordinary rape, gang rape, coercive sleep crawling, or marriage by capture or abduction could be motivated by anger, retaliation for rejection, or an attempt to "tame" a "haughty" girl. If the girl reported it to her kinsmen, they might beat up the boy, but public sanctions were negligible. Girls considered themselves valuable objects who could withhold sex altogether and always retained the right to pick and choose their lovers, a stance consistent with their valued status as sisters and daughters. All girls beautified themselves to enhance their sexual desirability, so that a haughty girl sent a contradictory message that was sexually provoking to men. Low-ranking girls were less controlled and more available sexually than elite girls, but boys and men in all ranks were expected to be sexually active, skilled, and successful.

ADOLESCENT CULTURE

The brother–sister relationship in Samoa involved almost complete avoidance. Siblings did not speak to one another, eat together, or sleep under the same roof, and sometimes might not even be allowed in the same room together. Above all, sex was never discussed when an opposite-sex sibling was nearby. This avoidance reflects the great respect mandated between brothers and sisters, which would be undermined by familiarity. In addition, brother–sister sexuality was a strict taboo, and the avoidance of direct communication lessened the chance of sibling incest. The eldest brother had to marry and reproduce for the lineage, but less pressure was put on junior brothers. As mentioned previously, not all boys remained with their descent group after marriage. Marriage would divide a junior brother's interest between his own group and that of his wife, so his marriage was often delayed, though ultimately younger brothers did marry and reproduce, adding members to their lineage.

Adolescent boys formed groups whose major interest was frequent sexual activity and talking about their affairs and sex in general. Girls spent time beautifying themselves, composing songs and entertainment, and engaging in pleasant amusements, sports, and games; they did little productive work. Adolescents often lived apart from their parents, in sex-segregated "dormitories," in separate residences in their parents' compounds, or in collective houses for young people. In yet another contradiction, the sexual activity of junior boys had to be invisible to society at large; thus it took place in dormitories, in the bush, or on the beach, and most properly in the dark and at night (Shore 1981:196). In Samoa, opposite-sex adolescents in a sexual relationship did not mix at all in public or during the day. The adolescent sexual culture was like sports or games, socially inconsequential but personally absorbing. In Samoa, sex was classified with other forms of play (Mead 1930:48).

Adolescent culture also emphasized that boys should sexually play the field, avoiding a strong attachment to any girl that might lead to an unwanted marriage. This low emotional involvement with members of the opposite sex, and in fact with any individual, was part of early childhood socialization (Mead 1973/1928); this supported the cohesiveness of siblings in contrast to that of a married couple or a couple in a nonmarital sexual relationship. Samoan husband–wife bonds were relatively weak, and adultery, divorce, and serial monogamy were common.

WHAT ABOUT LOVE? MARRIAGE AND CHILDREN

In Samoan sexual culture, sex and reproduction were considered basically masculine activities. The female was passive, a receptacle for, and a vehicle of, male sexual and procreative energy. In premarital relationships, a boy might declare that he would die if a girl refused him her sexual favors, but the Samoans laughed at stories of romantic love, scoffed at fidelity to a long absent wife, and believed that one love would quickly cure another. The composition of ardent love songs and flowery love letters seemed to suggest a Western concept of love, but in fact, a long-lasting passionate attachment to one person was rare (Mead 1973/1928:105).

Samoan marriages appeared "weakly motivated" and marital relations were secondary to the bond of biological kinship (Ortner 1981:386); as one ethnographer said, "marriage is a light garland" in

Polynesia (Danielsson 1956). Ideally, marriages should be arranged with careful negotiation and elaborate exchanges of both material goods (today cash is acceptable), but in fact most marriages were not arranged and were subject to little regulation. Marriage was mainly initiated by elopement, which was equivalent to kidnapping and emphasized a failure of the girl's brother to protect her chastity and fertility. But as the most convenient and least expensive form of marriage, elopement was eventually accepted by the girl's kin, particularly once a child was born.

The ascendancy of personal impulse over social arrangement in elopement degraded the wife's status. Similarly, an unmarried girl who was caught with a lover, a taupo who was not a virgin, or an unwed pregnant girl indicated the unacceptable triumph of personal desire, and the girl would be violently beaten by her brothers. Since both men and women inherited property and there was little gender exclusivity in domestic work, there was little economic motivation to marry or to stay married. Sexual ties within marriage were also weak. For unmarried men, sex was available with widows, divorced women, and unmarried girls (Mead 1973/1928). While sex with another man's wife was culturally disapproved of, high rates of adultery prevailed. There was also little restraint on the sexual freedom of divorced women. This might explain why husband and wife relationships in Polynesia were often described as "amiable" (Ortner 1981:87).

This amiability may also account for the high rate of adultery and divorce. Samoan marriages were sometimes called "brittle," which seems consistent with the general lack of deep emotional involvement between individuals, whether in sex or in friendship (Ortner 1981:387). In addition, a woman could always return to her kin group where she had land and she and her children were welcome. For young men, however, it was only through marriage that they could produce legitimate offspring, acquire status in their community as the head of a household, and gain aristocratic titles. And within the domestic realm, a husband/father had almost absolute authority and superiority over his wife and children. Given the seemingly low emotional ties between a married couple, jealousy was relatively rare in Samoa, though it appeared intense in other areas of Polynesia (Ortner 1981:389).

Reproduction was important to a woman's status, although the social role of parent was not, and parental functions were spread over a wide range of kin. In Samoa, mothers turned over the care of younger children to older children as soon as possible (Mead 1973/1928). Children were encouraged to see themselves as belonging to the wider kin group, and the universal Polynesian pattern of adoption and/or fosterage carried the same message. Samoan children were also free to wander off with no parental control, which might account for why the mother–child relationship, like marriage in Samoa, was often described as "amiable." Women as wives and mothers hardly appear in the ethnographic literature, which focuses on women as sisters and daughters.

CULTURAL CHANGE

Missionaries' arrival in Samoa produced some important changes in Samoan culture, forbidding "lascivious" night dancing, kava (an alcoholic drink) drinking, and polygynous marriage, all of which lowered the significance of the taupo and consequently, the importance of her virginity (Shankman 1996:560). Other cultural patterns, such as the love of pleasure, outspokenness in sexual matters, premarital sexual freedom, the traditional but mostly unrealized emphasis on virginity for unmarried girls, and the prevalence of adoption and common-law marriages remained (Shore 1981:197). Ultimately the chiefly form of political power disappeared and sexual privileges were no longer based on rank. The missionary influence also increased the emphasis on chastity, strict monogamy, and free choice rather than arranged marriages, an increase in nuclear families, and a more emotional definition of the word "love."

As this photograph from French Polynesia suggests, the European fantasies of the South Pacific continue to this day.

The modern expectation of romantic love as the basis of marriage has spread throughout the world through films, popular music, and commercial advertisements. Romantic love clearly exists in the Pacific Islands, although it is not an important traditional cultural pattern, and indeed contests much of what shapes gender relationships inside and outside of marriage. *Tanna*, a 2015 Australian film based on a true story of romance in Vanuatu, a remote Pacific island, describes how the romantic love a couple feels for each other complicates the very complex traditional arranged marriages and affects the whole society (Lindstrom 2016). Although arranged marriage is strongly resisted by many young people today, it still dominates island culture. Like Samoa, love in Vanuatu means to like, enjoy, or appreciate, and there is no requirement that husbands and wives should be "soul mates." While much traditional culture remains on Vanuatu, globalization is increasing through tourism, cell phones, and Christianity, although none of these appear in the film, reinforcing the still widespread perception of the South Pacific as an untouched paradise.

THE INFLUENCE OF MARGARET MEAD

Margaret Mead carried out her anthropological fieldwork in order to demonstrate the importance of culture in shaping human behavior, introducing cultural anthropology to the general public. She hoped that her description of the relatively easy life and sexual freedom of Samoan adolescents would motivate parents in the United States to socialize their children in ways that would reduce the stress and anxiety experienced by adolescent girls.

In 1983, anthropologist Derek Freeman published a book, *Margaret Mead and Samoa: The Making and Unmaking of an Anthropological Myth*, challenging the accuracy and reliability of Mead's ethnography. Thus ensued a heated debate among academics, Samoans, and the general public, which continues until today (Shankman 2013; Sullivan and Tiffany 2009; Tiffany 2009; Feinberg and Macphersen 2002; Feinberg 1988). Freeman contested almost all of Mead's findings, claiming she purposely lied, misinterpreted, or omitted important features of Samoan society, such as aggression, violence, stress, and sexual repression, which contradicted her conclusions about its easygoing culture.

Freeman's accusations have not persuaded most of the anthropological community, and indeed, Mead's ethnography does refer to many examples of these traits in Samoan culture (Feinberg 1988; Shankman 2009). Mead noted the many contradictions and ambiguities in Samoan society, some of which have been described in this chapter. In his aptly titled article, "Margaret Mead in Samoa: Coming of Age in Fact and Fiction," anthropologist Richard Feinberg (1988) notes that many of the accusations against Mead are perhaps inherent in ethnography. Every fieldworker omits some aspects of a culture in order to focus persuasively on his or her own major theme. This is particularly true when the anthropologist has a mission, like Mead, to convey cultural differences in a way that helps us rethink our own cultural assumptions. This, after all, is a central goal and a central achievement of cultural anthropology and indeed, is one of the purposes of this book.

1. Describe some of the central aspects of sexuality in Polynesia.
2. What do you think accounts for the important role of South Pacific culture in the "fantasies" of the West?
3. Summarize marriage and parental relationships in Samoa.
4. What role did love play in traditional Polynesian culture? How was it different from the role of "love" in Western culture?

Chapter Ten

Brothers Share a Wife
Fraternal Polyandry in the Himalayas

When I asked Dorje why he decided to marry with his two brothers rather than take his own wife, he thought for a moment, then said "it . . . [made it easier for] all of them to achieve a higher standard of living." When I asked Dorje's bride if it was difficult for her to cope with three brothers as husbands, she laughed and said she expected to be better off economically since she would have three husbands working for her and her children.

— Melvyn Goldstein (1987)

Fraternal polyandry, the marriage of one woman to several brothers, is rare and mainly exists in the high valleys of the Himalayan Mountains—in Tibet, Nepal, and India. The Nyinba of Nepal, an ethnically Tibetan population, is one of several Himalayan ethnic groups that practice fraternal polyandry. They are devout Buddhists who migrated to Nepal from Tibet when China annexed Tibet in the 1950s. Their culture, including ideas about sexuality, love, marriage, and kinship, is significantly shaped by Buddhism and thus differs from non-Buddhist polyandrous societies, such as those in India (Tiwari 2008).

The Nyinba economy, similar to other Himalayan communities, depends primarily on agriculture, herding, and long-distance trading in which grain, crafts, and herd animals are exchanged for salt and wool. Arable land is scarce and is owned by aristocratic families who are given land titles by the district authority. These families make up the highest social class; below them is a class of independent but economically marginal householders, and at the bottom is the landless peasant class of former slaves. Even though polyandry is outlawed in Nepal, it is practiced by most of the aristocratic landholding families with two or more sons; among the other classes, however, it is practically absent (Willett 1997; Levine 1988).

Economic roles within a polyandrous household are divided by sex; one brother always engages in agriculture, as the family both consumes and trades major crops such as buckwheat, wheat, barley, and millet. This brother may do the major preparatory plowing and planting, while the wife weeds the fields and processes the grain, which includes winnowing, husking, roasting and storing. The wife is solely responsible for child care and domestic chores, such as hauling water for the whole household and laundering all the family's clothes. Much of this work was previously done by slaves, and women's labor is considered similarly demeaning (Stockard 2002:88).

A second brother may specialize in small-scale cattle herding, mainly yaks and a few sheep, which meets the household's need for butter and meat. Animals are also occasionally traded. A third brother may engage in long-distance trading, the most lucrative aspect of the Nyinba economy. This brother travels to India and Tibet, which requires him to be absent from the household for months at a time. Thus, a family with three brothers is best able to ensure a household's prosperity. The Nyinba population of approximately 1,300 people occupies four villages in a previously isolated corner of northwest Nepal, which has now become more accessible and allows some Nyinba to have regular contact with outsiders (Levine 1988:xiii).

FRATERNAL POLYANDRY IN PRACTICE

Nyinba kinship is patrilineal and patrilocal, and fraternal polyandry is the most culturally valued form of Nyinba marriage, even though it is not universally practiced. Some families have only one son; aging or death of male members changes the household composition over time and sometimes one or more husbands may leave the family for personal reasons. Thus, between 1973 and 1983, the number of aristocratic families practicing fraternal polyandry declined from 100 percent to only 70 percent (Levine 1988:143). Some poor families, who cannot afford the high costs of a wedding and brideprice, encourage their eldest son to elope; in other poor families, one son may become a monk. This culture offers a significant contrast to other polyandrous Himalayan cultures, such as the Kinnauri of India, where polyandrous arranged marriages exist along with monogamy, marriage by capture, elopement, and love marriages (Tiwari 2008).

In the difficult Himalayan mountain environment, the fraternally polyandrous family is an important structure for survival.

In Nyinba fraternal polyandry all the brothers jointly wed a girl when the eldest son reaches maturity (Levine and Silk 1997:379). The eldest son is responsible for finding a wife, and while his preference may be considered, both his and the wife's parents must agree to the marriage. The eldest brother's horoscope is checked first against that of the wife. If they do not match, the girl's horoscope is checked against that of the second or perhaps a third brother, but if none of these matches, the marriage will be called off. The eldest brother arranges the brideprice, which is used by the bride's family to buy household goods that are brought to her new husbands' home. He also arranges for the wedding ceremony and takes a primary ritual role. Upon the marriage, all of the brothers in a family become co-husbands of the wife, and all of the children she bears will become part of the household. The ideal bride is a few years younger than the eldest brother, which, it is hoped, will ensure marital compatibility and result in the prompt production of heirs.

The eldest brother, called the "wife bringer," is the final authority for all family decisions. He controls the family estate, determines the allocation of cash income, decides how to divide the family's labor, and serves as the family representative in village political gatherings (Levine 1988:115). The eldest brother also initiates sexual activity with his wife. Despite the strong Nyinba ideal of strict sexual and emotional equality between all husbands and the wife, this sexual precedence often cements the eldest brother's power for the duration of the marriage. This special relationship, however, can generate tension, as it conflicts with the Nyinba ideal of equitable conjugal and procreative rights among the brothers.

SEXUAL ACCESS

A wife has a room of her own in which she always sleeps, [and] a husband's shoes left outside her door will signal his brother that he is too late and that [she is] already claimed for the evening.

— Stockard (2002)

Husbands and the wife have equal obligations to their family. Sexual favoritism is strongly discouraged. All the husbands must have equal sexual access to the wife and she must give them all a chance to father children. To facilitate sexual equity, a wife may spend an entire night with one husband at a time and rotate her sexual relations more or less equally. Because men are often away on trading trips, scheduling is flexible, and indeed probably accounts for the harmony in most polyandrous marriages. An unwritten Nyinba rule requires that a husband who has been away has first rights to spend the night with the wife on his return. Despite the ideal of sexual equity, however, a wife may give precedence to the eldest brother or another brother for whom she feels special affection, but no husband can be excluded from sexual activity (Levine 1988:164).

Among the Kinnauri of India, dyadic love marriages may become polyandrous later on and can also work harmoniously if the wife does not show sexual partiality (Tiwari 2008:130). In Nyinba society, if a wife avoids having sex with any of her husbands, she is branded as a "troublemaker" and a threat to family stability. A temporarily neglected husband is free to pursue extramarital affairs, although a wife may try to control the sexual activity of her favorite husband. The original closeness between a wife and the eldest husband may also change; as time passes, a wife may favor a younger husband who she previously treated like a child, but for whom she may now feel a greater sexual attraction.

In the joint household, a wife has her own room. Because of the openness of Nyinba sexual arrangements, decisions about having sexual relations are continually being made by either the husband or wife through subtle glances, words, or gestures. At night some women go to the bed of one of their husbands, but others prefer a husband to come to them. A husband who refuses sexual relations with his wife renounces all claims on his marriage rights. Both husbands and wives, however, are expected to meet their household obligations and all share equally in the economic benefits of their labor (Levine 1988:151).

SEX, LOVE, AND MARRIAGE

The natural desire in most men is to be in exclusive possession of their wives.

— Edward Westermarck (1925)

The Buddhist morality that shapes Nyinba ideas holds that the desire for earthly things, including sex and worldly love, are identified with material desire and denounced as greed, which interferes with the pursuit of salvation. Anger, greed, pride, and arrogance are subject to punishment, and theft and murder are punished by the law both in this world and in the hereafter (Levine 1981:2; Nyimba 1992). Adultery, though common, is considered a vice and if revealed, brings great shame to its participants (Levine 1981:110). Junior brothers most frequently engage in adultery, sometimes to test the field for a possible future marriage if they are dissatisfied with a wife or the division of her sexual favors. Wives less frequently engage in adultery than husbands, and if a wife has a tendency to commit adultery, this tendency declines after she bears children. If an adulterous wife is discovered, her male partner must pay a heavy fine, and she may be ejected from her household or even publically beaten. This contrasts with the much more open sexuality and emotional love that bind husbands and wives among the Kinnauri of India. Change is occurring, however, and this openness is decreasing somewhat among the younger generation, who are increasingly adopting stricter traditional Indian marriage ideology and practices.

The Nyinba have no word or concept to describe love, whether divine, parental, marital, or sexual. They identify the feelings between parents and children as a disinterested concern for "people they hold dear" and apply it most often to those who are weaker or more dependent. This value on nonattachment is central to Buddhism, because everything is impermanent. Extreme passion and sexual desire are viewed as undermining premarital chastity, marital fidelity, and family stability. Nyinba culture contains many cautionary tales illustrating the dangers of uncontrolled sexual passion. The community recognizes, however, that some people cannot control their passion, and as in other societies, this may be ignored, particularly for men, if it is done discreetly. Girls who engage in premarital sexual relations, however, are criticized as promiscuous, and in lower-class families such stigma may lead to elopement. As in other cultures, the Nyinba balance their responses to rule breaking with sympathy or sanctions depending on the circumstances.

Engaging in a passionate sexual relationship poses a dilemma for the individual. Violators of sexual norms may lose their "good name" in the community, and their actions can lead to personal unhappiness, social disruption, and even tragedy. Sometimes, in order to cement a love relationship between two unmarried people, a couple may take an oath to remain together as a "proof of sincerity" and an assurance of fidelity. The Nyinba claim that the oath checks the fickleness inherent in human nature, but it apparently is not always successful (Levine 1981:119).

Strong emotional ties are very important in maintaining Nyinba marriages, however. This creates a special dilemma for women. On the one hand, a wife is criticized for expressing emotional and sexual favoritism, but her economic security depends on a strong relationship with at least one husband, usually the eldest brother. Her position is strengthened when she bears sons, but she is very vulnerable if she does not bear children, if she bears only daughters, or if all her children die young. Some women react to this vulnerability by disguising their feelings, while others openly display their preference for one husband, even knowing this may lead to family breakup (partition). Partition causes particular suffering to a woman who can only leave the family with the children who are defined as belonging to the husband who leaves with her.

Most Nyinba divorces occur through the adulterous elopement of a wife; the only other alternative for a dissatisfied wife is to leave her husband's household and remain unmarried for three years. Few women choose this option, as it means living alone without adequate resources. Thus, it is most common for a dissatisfied wife to elope with another man, and her new husband must pay compensation to the husbands in her former household. Among the Nyinba, sexual entanglements and marital decisions present the individual with very difficult choices and are responsible for more social discord than any other factor in Nyinba social life (Levine 1981:124).

PATERNITY

Unlike some other systems of fraternal polyandry, as among the Kinnauri, the Nyinba put great value on determining a child's biological father. A husband designated as the one responsible for conception is identified as the "real" father (Levine and Silk 1997:379). The sexual precedence of the eldest brother with the wife gives him the opportunity to father most of the children born in the early years of the marriage. A wife confidently decides on the child's "real" father using the local understanding that women are considered most likely to become pregnant in the second week of their menstrual cycle (Levine 1988: 159). A woman's certainty is also enhanced by the fact that husbands are often away from home for long periods of time.

Nyinba husbands feel closer to sons identified as their own, and children develop closer ties to the husband designated as their "real" father, as well as to his other designated children. This is particularly important for sons. Biologically ascribed paternity partly determines inheritance; according to Nepali law, brothers inherit equally only from the man legally recognized as their father. If a polyandrous family breaks up, paternity may be designated by lot, by birth order (the first child being attributed to the eldest brother, the second child to the second eldest brother, and so on), by the closeness between the husband and wife, or by a decision based on the child's physical appearance (Levine 1988:168). Without a designated father, a child will be denied membership in a household; if it is a girl, there will be no one to pay her dowry. Men feel that their support for the household is more valuable if they have a child of their own to reap the benefits. They also fear that if they have no designated children there will be no one to look after them in their old age. The determination of paternity is not openly discussed, however, unless the family breaks up and a wife leaves with one of the brothers to form another household.

THE BREAKUP OF FAMILIES

Maintaining a stable family makes household management easier, confers a reputation as a good person on the household head, and raises a family's standard of living. Nevertheless, fraternal polyandry sometimes fails (Levine and Silk 1997). Though rare, partition may occur when there are great age differences among the husbands. Junior husbands may be dissatisfied with a much older wife and prefer to find a younger, more attractive woman for sexual relations (Levine 1988:166). Very occasionally a husband experiences sexual jealousy and prefers to leave the family and find another wife on his own. Younger brothers, particularly, may feel they are not treated equally and resent being dominated by their elder siblings. Some men may have unsatisfactory interpersonal and sexual relationships with their wife, particularly where the wife is much older (Goldstein 1978:328). Still, other brothers, especially in a large family, may have unmet expectations regarding their opportunities for designated paternity.

If a man's satisfaction in marriage has reproductive consequences, as claimed by evolutionary biologists, a husband who is much younger than his wife may be concerned about her ability to bear his children in the future. This may explain the data indicating that eldest brothers initiate the fewest partitions, and younger brothers initiate the most partitions (Levine and Silk 1997:382). When Nyinba men are asked directly about what causes partition, they mainly mention the large size of their sibling group, a lack of closeness among the husbands, insufficient landholdings, difficulties in the interpersonal relationship between the husband and the wife, or the absence of children designated as one's own (Levine 1988:257).

EXPLAINING POLYANDRY

One reason for this most odious custom is the sterility of the soil . . . if brothers form separate families they would be reduced to beggary.

— Jesuit Ippolito Desideri (Fillipi 1937)

Westerners, including cultural anthropologists, have long considered fraternal polyandry as exotic and unnatural, and heated theoretical debates on its origins and persistence continue in the academic literature (Cassidy and Lee 1989). The strong Western and specifically Christian values on marital sexual exclusivity and biologically based paternity, as well as a male bias in the social sciences, focusing on male jealousy, underlie these views. Both biological and materialistic explanations have been used to explain Himalayan fraternal polyandry and to account for its expected disappearance. A Darwinian perspective, emphasizing the importance of male reproductive success, holds that sharing a wife and uncertainties about paternity would exist only in the most strained economic conditions.

The ecologically difficult environment of the Himalayan Mountains strongly supports materialist theories, which view fraternal polyandry as particularly adaptive to this environment and also particularly effective in slowing population growth (Tiwari 2008; Childs 2003; Willett 1997; Goldstein 1987). When economic collectivization, mandated by the Chinese government from the 1960s to the 1980s, was dismantled, an emphasis on individual initiative emerged. This led to a revival of fraternal polyandry, which persists to this day (Childs, Goldstein, and Wangdui 2011). Some ethnographic research, however, challenges these exclusively materialistic views. This research observes the great importance the Nyinba attach to their culture, particularly to fraternal polyandry (Levine 1988). Indeed, statistical data on the partition of Nyinba polyandrous marriages do not support the view that economic factors are determinant, though they are important (Levine and Silk 1997:385).

The Nyinba explanation for the persistence of polyandry is the importance of the salt trade to their economy; this trade can only be done by men. They admit, however, that keeping the family size small is also important in maintaining family stability. Men are more satisfied with polyandrous families containing only two or three brothers than with larger households. Younger brothers, especially, find the constraints on their sexual activity in larger families burdensome, and much older wives unsatisfactory. And, as Tiwari's personal narratives of Kinnauri families illustrate, several husbands in a family greatly complicate husband–wife relationships.

Due to economic and political changes, and Christian missionary influence, fraternal polyandry is declining in many areas of the Himalayan Mountains. Agriculture and trade, for example, are now less lucrative because of competition with neighboring countries like China and India. In some areas, however, fraternal polyandry is not only stable but may even be reviving. Some polyandrous families in Tibet have realized that if their sons set up independent households, the family landholdings will be divided and gone within a few generations. In addition, having several husbands in a family makes it easier to take advantage of new economic opportunities, such as earning cash as urban migrant laborers and working on rural construction sites (Goldstein 1987). In addition, while unmarried daughters were previously considered a burden, with increasing opportunities for education and small businesses, and improvements in transportation, they now have value as a source of both income and care for their aging parents (Childs, Goldstein, and Wangdui 2011).

All Himalayan societies are undergoing change. Due to the increasingly scarce and the rising price of handwoven goods, many Nyinba are buying imported cotton and corduroy, and some younger Nyinba even wear Western clothing. Despite the attraction of young people to modern dress, the Nyinba are deeply committed to their traditional garments, hairstyles, and jewelry, which are unique, elaborate, and central to their religious ceremonies.

Schools have opened in the Nyinba region, and while these are mostly attended by boys, some girls are also being educated, which may have a cultural or social impact (Levine 1988:224). Although the Nyinba maintain contact with neighboring ethnic groups, they persist in their deep commitment to their ethnically unique culture, including the practice of fraternal polyandry. The Nyinba strongly believe that kinship is the only trustworthy basis for individual and community well-being and view fraternal polyandry as the most important basis of men's cooperation and economic success.

While population increase has impoverished many communities in Nepal, the Nyinba have maintained a slow rate of population growth due to fraternal polyandry (Childs 2003). Very few Nyinba migrate from their villages and only a few immigrants have joined their community. The Nyinba remain highly satisfied with their small world. The persistence of their culture reminds us that even the rare system of fraternal polyandry, which requires sexual and reproductive sacrifices, survives as much for cultural reasons as it does because of economic adaptation.

1. Briefly describe what distinguishes fraternal polyandry from other forms of marriage.
2. What are some of the most adaptive functions of fraternal polyandry?
3. What seems to be the major reasons for the breakup of polyandrous marriages?
4. Can you imagine yourself in a polyandrous marriage? Why or why not?

Chapter Eleven

Same-Sex Relationships
Variations in Sexuality, Love, and Marriage

Anthropological ethnographies are a testimony to the complexity and diversity of sexuality, sex, and gender around the world. Same-sex relationships, which incorporate romantic or sexual attraction or sexual activity between members of the same sex, vary widely in different cultures and different historical periods (Ackroyd 2018). Some societies disparage and stigmatize same-sex relationships, while other societies ignore them, accept them, or value them above other relationships. The vast literature on sexuality generally indicates that sexual orientation occurs due to a complex interplay of genetic, hormonal, and environmental influences. In some societies, such as the Sambia and the Gebusi of New Guinea, sexual activity between males plays an important role in traditional male initiation (Knauft 2016; Herdt 1987). The culture of both societies holds that males cannot achieve reproductive competence without semen, which is not naturally produced but must be artificially introduced into the body. Thus, an essential part of male initiation is for boys to consume semen from adult men through fellatio. Only in this way can boys become "strong men," capable of becoming fathers and vigorous warriors. This cultural pattern is similar in some ways to that of ancient Greece and Rome, as we see below.

Most of the historical and ethnographic evidence regarding same-sex attraction has focused on males rather than females. This may be due to a weaker interest in women's sexuality in patriarchal cultures or to a male academic bias in research in the past.

ANCIENT GREECE AND ROME

O soft and dainty maiden, from afar
I watch you, as amidst the flowers you move
And pluck them, singing
More golden than all gold your tresses are
Never was harp-note like your voice, my love,
Your voice sweet singing.

— Sappho

With the rise of feminist theory since the late twentieth century, there has been a renewed interest in erotic relations between women, both in ancient times and today (Rabinowitz and Auanger 2008; Blackwood and Wieringa 1999). Sappho, a seventh century B.C.E. Greek poet from the island of Lesbos (from which the term **lesbian** derives), is the major source of references to women's same-sex relationships in the ancient world. Sappho wrote emotionally powerful poetry about the passionate love between women, and she appealed to Aphrodite, the goddess of love, for help in her own love relationships with women. The poetry of Sappho and the other women she influenced did not emphasize the hierarchy between the beloved and the lover as in poetry written by men but described erotic desires based on equality and mutuality. The classical Roman narrative, Ovid's *Metamorphoses*, featured the agonies of female same-sex desire and challenged Roman notions of male sexual activism and female sexual passivity.

The relative lack of evidence for lesbian relationships in ancient Greece and Rome is partly due to a cultural ideology in which male sexuality dominated and female sexuality was repressed. Women's gender roles mainly were related to their social status, which was determined by their fathers and husbands. And because chastity was the dominant value regarding women's sexuality, their nonconforming erotic lives were largely hidden.

Male same-sex eroticism was much more out in the open. Even early Greek Christianity did not oppose male same-sex sexual relationships and actually celebrated a same-sex commitment ceremony between two openly gay Christian saints, Saint Sergius and Saint Bacchus, in 303 C.E. (Feldman 2013). As Christianity expanded, it became less open to same-sex relations and by the 1400s, Christian churchmen described Sappho as a "whore," branded her work as deviant due to her "unnatural love of women," and destroyed much of her written legacy.

In ancient Greece (600 B.C.E.), male same-sex erotic desires and relationships were considered superior to heterosexual sexual relations. Gay relationships mainly involved adolescent boys and older men. Age and generation were important markers of social status and cultural knowledge: passionate and companionate erotic encounters were a way of introducing masculine roles to boys. Greek culture emphasized the culturally significant relationship between warrior same-sex eroticism and masculinity, requiring that the older male play the active sexual role and the younger male the passive role. As long as this distinction was upheld, the relationship did not feminize or dishonor the boy. Indeed, to the contrary, the relationships were celebrated by the boy's family and community with gifts and feasts. In Greek culture, male strength, honor, virility, courage, beauty, and nobility were central, symbolized by both the athlete and the warrior. The younger male's consent was required for all relations. These relationships did not replace marriage; achieving adult identity required marrying and fathering children. The individuals in these relationships were not considered "gay"; the emphasis was on doing rather than being, on practice rather than identity, in contrast to the ideology which has, until most recently, dominated Western culture (Herdt 1997:69).

MODERN TIMES

The shift to love as the dominant reason for marriage in the United States . . . has allowed for the widespread shift to gay marriage, which is based on love and therefore viewed as another option to heterosexual love. Gay marriage, in turn, reinforces the concept of romantic love as the chief reason for heterosexual marriage.

— Douglas Feldman

Michel Foucault's 1976 publication of the history of sexuality illustrates the dramatic changes in Western ideas about same-sex intimacy, mainly regarding men but also regarding women. Since the twelfth century, sodomy, defined as anal intercourse between men and also between a man and a woman, was a crime punished by both religious and secular authorities. For several centuries criminal trials for sodomy proliferated; later, women's same-sex relationships were also criminalized.

Between the late 1800s and the early 1900s, England, France, and the Netherlands treated same-sex liaisons as a stigmatized and criminalized role of the sodomite (Herdt 1997; Trumbach 1993; Hekma 1993). Sodomites were considered "sexual beasts," and there was little recognition that affection or love played any role in these relationships. But letters between two men in a sexual relationship from this period indicate that these relationships were not only about sex but also about love (van der Meer 1993: 164–165).

Both the Hebrew and the Christian Testaments condemn same-sex relationships as sinful and unnatural. Antisodomy laws, applying to anal and oral sex between men and oral sex between women, were incorporated into English common law and subsequently into the law of the United States. These laws applied to both gay and heterosexual couples. The laws were rarely enforced, but stigmatizing cultural attitudes toward same-sex relationships resulted in concealing such relationships; these laws did provide a basis for discriminatory exclusion, for example, in the military and other areas of life and culture. Up until 2015, neither federal nor state laws legalized same-sex marriages, depriving couples of financial and other benefits and of the cultural acceptance accorded to married heterosexual couples.

GAY MARRIAGE

By the early twentieth century, with increasing urbanization, gay, and later lesbian, subcultures became more open in the United States. A "gay rights" movement activated by the 1969 Stonewall rebellion in New York City ultimately led to widespread activist protests demanding that "gay marriage" be legalized. In 1976 the United States Supreme Court had denied rights to a male couple in Virginia (*Doe v. Commonwealth's Attorney for City of Richmond*). The court held that Virginia's antisodomy laws were valid and that the privacy rights claimed by the couple, who had been subject to a police raid, applied only to heterosexual couples. In 1986 the Supreme Court again ruled against a male couple's right to privacy, in an antisodomy case in Georgia (*Bowers v. Hardwick*). Chief Justice Warren Burger claimed, "The proscriptions against sodomy are . . . firmly rooted in Judeo-Christian moral and ethical standards. . . . To hold that the act of homosexual sodomy is somehow protected as a fundamental right would be to cast aside millennia of moral teaching" (quoted in Norgren and Nanda 2006:183–185).

Gay activism continued, however, and in 2003, the Supreme Court found for the male defendants in a Texas antisodomy case (*Lawrence v. Texas*) where the law applied only to same-sex couples. The court held that the Texas law violated the defendants' rights (their home was also subject to a police raid) under the Due Process Clause of the Fourteenth Amendment of the United States Constitution.

These cases ultimately paved the way for gay marriage: In 2013, the LGBT activist, Edith Windsor, who had married her female partner in Canada in 2007, sued for the right to receive the tax benefits she had been denied at her partner's death, which were available to heterosexual couples. In *US v. Windsor*, the Supreme Court ruled in her favor, but the decision applied only to 13 states and the District of

One of the most important goals of the modern gay activist movement is the legalization of gay marriage worldwide.

Columbia. Two years later, however, in *Obergefell v. Hodges*, the Supreme Court ruled that same-sex couples had a constitutional right to marry anywhere in the United States and were entitled to all the protections and privileges of heterosexual couples (McFadden 2017). Over the past 40 years, public approval of same-sex marriage has increased in the United States. In 2018, two male helicopter pilots celebrated their marriage with full military fanfare at the West Point Military Academy (Mallozzi 2018).

Same-sex couples in the United States continue to experience discrimination, however. In 2018, the Supreme Court upheld the rights of a cake shop owner who refused to make a wedding cake for a gay couple's wedding because his religion disapproved of gay marriage. This decision, in *Masterpiece Cakeshop v. Colorado Civil Rights Commission*, was narrowly based on hostile remarks made by some commission members regarding the baker's religion; it suggests, however, that future decisions may also uphold similar cases of discrimination, based on the importance of religious liberty, which is central to the First Amendment of the United States Constitution (Posner 2018).

With the legalization of same-sex marriage in the United States, same-sex marriage has now become an international issue. Other nations that have followed suit include Austria, Australia, Germany, Taiwan, and most of mainland Great Britain. Bills and referendums for same-sex marriage are now up for consideration in India, Costa Rica, and Romania among other places. For some people, same-sex marriage is mainly a human rights issue; for others, support for same-sex marriage is the more personal desire to make a public commitment to "someone you love" (Maxwell 2017).

But some global trends are opposing LGBTQ rights, particularly since the devastating AIDS epidemic, which was widely believed to have originated in gay communities, though it is now taking its toll among both gay and heterosexual couples throughout the world (Feldman 2010; Hirsch and Wardlow 2006). In Vladimir Putin's Russia and in the Russian Republic of Chechnya, the state has launched all-out assaults on LGBTQ people, arresting and torturing hundreds in secret prisons. The Egyptian government has also intensified an ongoing and widespread crackdown on the LGBTQ community, subjecting some individuals to barbaric rectal examinations and sentencing others to long prison terms. The nations of Georgia, Tanzania, Tajikistan, Turkey, and Bangladesh have also attacked LGBTQ people, and violence against gays and lesbians now occurs in Brazil, Uganda, and Canada, in addition to the United States.

LESBIAN RELATIONSHIPS IN INDONESIA

If there is no feeling . . .

— Wieringa (2007)

Indonesia has been moving toward stricter sanctions on gay rights, gatherings, and pro–gay rights rhetoric. The Family Love Alliance, an antigay group, argues that the influence of the gay community is spreading, particularly since the United States legalized same-sex marriage, resulting in "moral degradation" (*New Straits Times* 2017).

Indonesia's political and popular culture now more ardently supports a national ideology that stresses Indonesian cultural unity, social consensus, and traditional values. These ideas conflict with the international gay and feminist rights movements, which are now easily accessed through the internet. This government policy makes life more difficult for gay men and even more so for lesbians, as the normative gender roles for Indonesian women are defined as that of passive, subservient wife and mother.

Saskia Wieringa's (2007) moving ethnography of a community of socially and economically marginalized feminist lesbians living on the outskirts of Jakarta, Indonesia's largest city, demonstrates how these women negotiate their love and sexuality in a daily struggle between the national ideology, the global discourse supporting women's rights, including sexual rights, and their own tenuous social position. This is a "butch–femme" community in which each of the partners takes on the normative gender role of Indonesian heterosexual couples, with those taking the male role (the "butch") defining themselves as having a man's soul in a woman's body. They sport masculine haircuts, wear masculine clothing, and exhibit masculine body language and speech. The "femme" partner in the couple claims "sexual normalcy" as wives of their butch husbands. They try to act out the Indonesian cultural ideal of a wife's role, engaging in the normal domestic activities of married women and participating in women's neighborhood voluntary associations. Most of the couples Wieringa studied live together, and a few couples have even adopted a child.

Both partners in committed relationships in this community declare that the erotic impulse is the main motivation in the choice of their same-sex partner, stressing the importance of the enduring bonding of souls and bodies that a love relationship entails. As the chapter's opening quote suggests, these couples hold that emotional feeling is central to their relationships. They embrace the "fierce passion" of "the culture of love," which is not only a "modern" idea but also one widespread in Indonesia, inspired by the traditional Javanese Hinduised court culture described in Hindu religious epics.

The lesbian couples in Wieringa's study generally lack advanced education and stable income, both of which negatively affect their personal relationships. If the butch partner is financially unable to play the male role, he feels dishonored and may become jealous of his wife, especially if the wife works outside the home. The complete loyalty of the partners in this lesbian relationship is central to their bond. The self-definition of the butch partner as having a man's soul makes some butches reluctant about joining the emerging women's rights movement, which criticizes gender role inequality in Indonesian marriages. Many butch–femme couples feel more comfortable conforming to the dominant Indonesian cultural ideology that includes the idea of romantic love and in which possessiveness, jealousy, women's oppression, and male superiority are valued. At the same time, femme wives are widely believed to sexually seduce their husbands; butch husbands claim that it is part of their masculine honor to satisfy the desires of their partners, and jealousy of a wife's outside relationship is seen as a sign of love (Wieringa 2007:79). The lower-class butch and femme lesbians express their relationships more openly than do the well-educated, upper-class lesbians. Although upper-class lesbians are connected to internet lesbian groups and have other international lesbian connections, lesbians in this class do not openly live together as couples and do not "come out" publically.

The international women's rights movement, which promotes greater individual choice of one's partner and the expansion of romantic love, does not easily fit Indonesian butch–femme relationships. Rather, Indonesian butch–femme couples are less motivated by the global movement—which they, in fact, have little contact with—and instead base their relationships on the various traditions of Indonesians who identify as transgender, on the national ideology of romantic love, on and the culture of public silence about sexuality. Wieringa's ethnography demonstrates the need to consider specific cultural processes and contexts in explaining the role of love and companionate marriage. It also requires us to rethink the Western theory that love as the basis of marriage is a uniform response to the influence of the West and, particularly, of the United States.

SEX, LOVE, AND MARRIAGE AMONG INDIAN HIJRAS

Marriage . . . is not [just] sexual desire . . . it is a companion through life. . . . It is companionship and the hope that the person will be there with you later.

— Gayatri Reddy (2006)

Hijras are most popularly defined in India as "neither man nor woman," although activist groups now include them in the modern cross-cultural umbrella of **transgender**, persons who identify themselves differently from the sex/gender role they were assigned at birth. Hijras identify with the many gender roles described in ancient Hindu mythology. They are born as males and undergo emasculation (castration). Many have no sexual desire or sexual relationships. This identity endows them with the power to grant fertility to others: their traditional ritual roles are to perform skits and sing songs at weddings and to offer blessings when a child is born. Hijras also identify themselves as women; they dress in women's clothing, wear their hair long like women, and pluck and shave their facial and body hair. Hijra rules require them to live in specifically hijra communities governed by their elders, but some hijras live on their own, or with a man they define as their husband (Hossain 2012; Reddy 2005; Nanda 1999).

Hijras do have sexual desires for men; some recent research in fact includes these desires as central to hijra identity (Hossain 2012). Hijras do also fall in love and may even "marry" husbands who are not hijras but heterosexual men. Many hijras express a very strong desire for emotional intimacy and companionate marriage, as indicated in the quotation above. The marital ideal stressing the relationship between sexuality, intimacy, and marriage is now widely expressed in modern Indian popular culture through films, television, advertising, and magazines, and the hijras negotiate this ideal in their own way.

Contrary to their community rules, hijras very often engage in prostitution because both sexual desire and money are important to many hijras. As one hijra prostitute exclaimed, "we mainly do this sex work because of [our] desire for men . . . and to earn money of course!. . . But there is a fondness for sex . . . I do not lie." She further claimed that all hijras sexually desire men, even those who are not sex workers. Hijra prostitutes expose themselves to many difficulties: the threat of arrest, eviction from or destruction of their homes, and disrespect in their community. In spite of these difficulties, they continue to engage in sex work, mainly for money—it is not unusual to have six or eight clients in one night—but also, equally as important to them, for sexual pleasure and enjoyment (Reddy 2006:189).

Contrary to popular stereotypes, hijras do have sexual desires for men, they fall in love and one important hijra goal is a loving, companionate marriage, as illustrated by this couple.

Many hijra sex workers say their customers can appease their sexual desires, but the caring and companionship offered by intimate relationships with their husbands are more important to their happiness. Despite the frequency of hijra sex work, a hijra who considers herself married holds up a lifelong commitment to her husband as an ideal. Hijras define a good husband as one who visits his hijra wife frequently, brings her small gifts, takes care of her if she is ill, and does not hide his relationship with her from his family. A "bad" husband comes to see his hijra wife only when he wants money for alcohol and is often drunk and violent and even beats his wife. Hijra conversations repeatedly indicate the importance of openness, caring, and trust as criteria for a good husband (Reddy 2006:184). One hijra, describing how her husband violently beat her, said she did not leave him because there was a bond of love between them. This lifelong love, caring, and emotional intimacy is the central factor in hijra marriages, irrespective of their engaging in sex work with many partners.

In their marriages, hijras (like the butch–femmes in Indonesia) explicitly follow normative Indian gender roles, with the hijra wife carrying out the domestic duties of cooking and cleaning, never acting promiscuous in public, and always looking after her husband and his needs. Although their marital relationships may involve violence and abuse from a hijra's husband, they hardly ever consider fighting back.

"How could we do that? He is our husband!" As Reddy somewhat sadly concludes (2006:190), the longing bonds of affection and emotional intimacy that motivate the hijras' "eternal quest" for the ideal husband also account for the daily pathos and difficulties of their lives.

The increasing knowledge of the many variant sex and gender roles existing in non-Western and Western societies is evidence of a global community that is not just about sex but also includes romantic love and companionate marriage.

A NOTE ON TERMINOLOGY

The vast literature indicating the diverse nature of same-sex and same-gender relationships is indicated by expansion and change in variant sex and gender terminology (Besnier 2018; Winter 2015; Rind 2015; Nanda 2014; Herdt 1997). Some terminology changes are directed at normalizing same-sex desire and practices: "homosexual," for example, is no longer used as a noun or an adjective. The term **transsexual** implies the use of medical treatments by an individual who wishes to change from his or her sex at birth to the opposite sex. The category of transsexual supports the traditional Western binary of sex and gender: male and female, man and woman, although the term transsexual has now largely been incorporated into the category of transgender (Bolin 1993). The term cross-dresser typically refers to heterosexual men who occasionally wear women's clothes, makeup, and jewelry, but cross-dressing is also a form of diversity among males, females, and intersexed individuals in some Native American cultures (Roscoe 1998) and may refer to "drag queens" when engaged in for the purposes of entertainment (Newton 1979).

1. In what ways, if any, has this chapter changed or clarified your ideas about human sexuality?
2. What future do you anticipate for same-sex relationships and communities?
3. Discuss your reactions to the same-sex relationships described in this chapter.
4. What, if any, appear to be some differences in the relations between the same-sex couples described here and heterosexual couples?

Chapter Twelve

Romantic Love and Marriage
Similarities and Differences in a Changing World

The topics discussed in each chapter were chosen with an eye to representing a wide range of cultural patterns regarding love and marriage throughout the world. Marriage is found in almost all human societies because of its many adaptive functions in widely diverse environments. Romantic love also appears to be universal, but it is not the basis of marriage in most societies. A central theme of this book is the various ways that romantic love as a basis for marriage has, over time, become more widespread across cultures. This phenomenon is integrated in different societies in different ways, depending on local contexts and global connections.

As the chapters illustrate, some sources of change regarding romantic love as the basis of marriage are related to economic requirements and interests; urban and transnational migration; the expanding role of Christianity; Western popular culture accessed through television, films, and the internet; the global expansion of online dating and marriage sites; the growing importance of the value of individual freedom; the desire to achieve a "modern" identity; and changes in gender ideologies. Space limitations preclude analyzing all of these topics for each society discussed in the text; here I suggest only some of the examples of change in different cultures and the ways in which they are both similar to and different from each other.

NUMBER OF SPOUSES

The number of spouses permitted is an important aspect of marriage. Monogamy, which is the only legal form of marriage in Western societies, including the United States, is also characteristic of Hindu India, the People's Republic of China, and Brazil, a Catholic nation influenced by European culture. Many African societies, such as the Igbo, permit polygyny (multiple wives), and Islamic law permits four wives. Among the Igbo, polygyny is decreasing, partly because few men can support several wives; the majority of Muslim men have one wife for the same reason. The introduction of romantic love into Nigerian and Islamic societies, as well as urbanization, has led to a decline of polygynous marriages. Among the Igbo, the establishment of Christianity also resulted in the decline of polygyny. Polyandry, or multiple husbands, is very rare; it is mainly found among Himalayan ethnic groups, and both Nepal and China have attempted to outlaw it. Polyandry is mainly adaptive to a scarcity of land. As more Himalayan societies became "modern," and left agriculture to engage in other economic pursuits, polyandry appeared to be in decline, though it now seems stabilized and even on the rise as an important element of traditional Himalayan culture.

ROMANTIC LOVE AND MARITAL STABILITY

One pattern that seems universal is that romantic love as the basis for marriage is very often an ideal but not the reality for many couples. One indication of this disconnect is the high and, in many cultures, increasing rate of divorce. This is true for the United States, as well as for India, although the divorce rate there is still very low. Romantic love plays a role in the rate of partition in Himalayan polyandrous families, where a wife may abandon her original husbands to marry a lover. Thus, although the United States and the Nyinba represent extreme examples of different marriage systems, the result of romantic love is somewhat similar in both cultures. There is also a big difference, however: in the United States, divorce is motivated by the dying out of romantic love in a marriage, while among the Nyinba, it is motivated by the romantic attachment to another man outside a polyandrous marriage. The connection between romantic love and companionate marriage in the Brazilian favela is also unstable, as the poverty of the favela makes it very difficult to incorporate this modern ideology into an economic system that deprives men of the stable incomes needed to support a family.

CHOOSING A MATE

In practically all societies outside of the West, kin-group interests rather than individual desires are the basis of mate selection. Parents, and other kin of the bride and groom, play a central, even determinative role in selecting spouses for their children. We have seen this most clearly in China and India. Traditionally arranged marriages dominated both cultures, but this practice is slowly changing. Again, because of the similarities between China and India—both are basically rural agricultural societies—romantic love played almost no role in marriage. With the increase of modern economies in both societies, however, as well as increasing urbanization, migration to the West, and access to the internet, romantic love has become widespread. The view that individual choice is destroying the traditional extended family in India and China is highly exaggerated, however. In both societies features of arranged as well as "love marriages" are frequently integrated into the modern middle class.

The internet and global marriage sites, the diffusion of popular Western media, and the growth of national media portraying romantic love in a positive way, contribute to the desire to incorporate romantic love into marriage, not just in China and India, but also in the Brazilian favela, among the Igbo, and even in remote societies in the South Pacific. Romantic love matches, however, often mean financial difficulties for young families in China, India, Nigeria, and Brazil, and the need for financial help from kin has sustained the importance of the kin group in marital choice. In remote South Pacific cultures, romantic love also poses a threat to the strict rules of marriage exchange and can result in great individual unhappiness and social turmoil. Even in the United States, where family agreement is not necessary, most young couples marry within their racial, ethnic, and class categories, making parental approval more likely. This is changing somewhat, however, as interracial and interethnic marriages are increasing.

KINSHIP AND GENDER ROLES

Most of the world's societies are patrilineal, patriarchal, and patrilocal, as is true of all but one of the cultures (the Minangkabau) described in this book. This kinship pattern is consistent with highly differentiated gender role identity and activities: men dominate economically, while women primarily engage in domestic activities and the care of children. This division also generally awards more power to men, even in supposedly egalitarian Western societies, including the United States.

However, as women become more educated and increase their paid work outside the home, this pattern is changing. Consistent with the increase of romantic love, individual choice of mates, the rise of nuclear families, and a "modern" identity, gender roles throughout the world are becoming more egalitarian, as is noted for China, India, Brazil, Nigeria, and Iran.

Even as gender roles become more egalitarian, however, the power of women is much greater in matrilineal societies, such as the Na of China and the Minangkabau of Indonesia. In both cases, these ethnic groups are a minority in their societies and strongly contrast with the dominant patterns of the nation-states they reside in. In some ethnic groups in West Africa, women also have substantial power, though nowhere does it reach the power of the matrilineal Minangkabau. The introduction of romantic love in Minangkabau society, along with the strong support of the Indonesian Muslim government for the nuclear patriarchal family, has not resulted in the disappearance of matriliny but has made this practice more unstable. Nor has gender egalitarianism affected most lesbian relationships in Indonesia; the "butch–femme" relationship, based on strong emotional feeling, retains the culturally dominant patriarchal gender relations of the Islamic nuclear family.

THE ROLE OF ECONOMICS, POLITICS, AND RELIGION

Despite the growing role of romantic love in marriage, the exchange of material goods is still almost universal in confirming a marital relationship. The roles of bridewealth and dowry, in the form of material goods or cash, remain central in China, India, and among the Igbo. Dowry is illegal in India but is still essential in most arranged and even love marriages; indeed, the extreme consumerism and desire for upward mobility in the middle class have resulted in a rise in "dowry deaths," in both rural and urban families. As many national economies become more insecure and consumerism emerges as critical to romantic relationships, both inside and outside of marriage, material exchanges do not disappear but become a source of tension.

Politics, in the form of the important legal and cultural role of the state, also affects the incorporation of romantic love as the basis of marriage. The earlier Communist government of the People's Republic of China officially gave its stamp of approval to marriage based on the emotional and companionate tie between individuals, and the present government has increasingly opened up its culture to globalization through internet dating and marriage sites. Due to a shortage of females, China also encourages marriage between Chinese men and women from other nations. In Indonesia, we have seen the important role of the state in fostering companionate marriages among the Minangkabau, as well as throughout the country. The United States has recognized the importance of romantic love in legalizing same-sex marriage, as have many other nations, though not China, India, or Iran. The role of the state here is critical; without legalization, same-sex relationships must remain outside the cultural norm and are more likely to experience various forms of discrimination. In Iran, the state wields control in repressing freedom regarding sexuality and the expression of romantic love; the "sexual revolution" continues, however, as well as the protests for more freedom for women, abetted by their increasing education and participation in the Iranian economy.

Religion also plays a central role in promoting romantic love as the basis of marriage, most obviously, perhaps, in the Islamic state of Indonesia but also as a result of Christian missionaries, as in the South Pacific and among the Igbo. The Buddhist religion, on the other hand, as we see in Tibet, dismisses romantic love as equivalent to greed and warns how dangerous such emotions can be both for the individuals as well as for the larger society. And the U.S. Supreme Court's ruling that a baker, due to his religious beliefs, has the right not to supply a wedding cake for a gay couple indicates the influence of religion regarding gay marriage in this society.

In conclusion, it seems clear that the expansion of worldwide global connections, as well as local changes regarding economics, politics, and culture, exerts significant pressure for changes in sexuality, love, marriage, family, and gender identities and roles throughout the world.

1. What appears to be the most important source of change regarding the spread of romantic love and companionate marriage in diverse cultures?
2. The ideal of romantic love and companionate marriage is often not matched by the reality. What are some examples of this disjunction in different cultures?
3. In what ways does the nation-state affect the incorporation of romantic love and companionate marriage into a culture?
4. How is romantic love as a basis for marriage related to the stability of marriage and society? Give examples from different cultures.
5. What are some of the relationships between gender, social organization, marriage patterns, and the role of romantic love in a society?
6. What are the important elements of globalization that affect the acceptance, spread, and role of romantic love and companionate marriage? Give examples from the text.

Glossary

Affinal Kin: kin related through ties of marriage.

Bilateral (kinship system): mother's and father's kin are both culturally acknowledged as the source of kinship relations and obligations.

Bridewealth (also called bride-price): gifts or cash given by the groom's family to the bride's family to seal a marriage.

Carnival: an annual festival held in Brazil (and other nations) at the beginning of Lent, involving huge parades and samba dancing.

Caste: the endogamous unit in the Indian caste system which is based on birth and hierarchically structured.

Chiefdom: an independent political unit incorporating multiple communities under the permanent control of a paramount chief.

Companionate Marriage: marriage based on a strong individual, emotional, sexual, and social relationship between spouses.

Cross cousins: the children of the father's sister or the mother's brother

Culture: the learned behaviors and symbols shared by a group of people which guides their lives as members of a particular society.

Dowry: gifts or cash given by a bride's family to the groom's family on marriage.

Endogamy: the requirement that people marry within a certain group.

Ethnocentrism: the view people have that their own culture is natural and right.

Exogamy: the requirement that people marry outside a certain group.

Extended Family: two or more generations living in the same household

Fieldwork: an anthropologist's long-term stay among the people he or she is studying.

Fraternal Polyandry: several brothers married to one wife.

Gender: a cultural construction attached to the differences between sexes.

Gender Roles: the cultural patterns and activities associated with sex differences.

Heterosexual(ity): an erotic relationship between males and females

Incest Taboos: rules that prohibit sexual relations between specified kin, such as parents and children or between siblings.

Kinship System: the culturally based rules for specifying the structure of blood and other relationships in a society.

Lesbians: women who engage in same-sex relationships.

Lineage: a group of kin whose members trace descent from a common ancestor.

Marriage: the customs, rules, and regulations that establish a special relationship between sexually cohabiting adults, between them and any children for whom they take responsibility, and between the kin of the married couple.

Matriarchy: a society in which women have the most power and status.

Matrilineal: links between kin are determined by the female line.

Matrilocal: society in which a man lives in his wife's house after marriage.

Monogamy: only one spouse at a time permitted in marriage.

Neolocal: a married couple living separately from their kin in their own household.

Nuclear Family: a family consisting of two spouses and their children.

Parallel Cousins: the children of a father's brother or a mother's sister.

Patriarchy: a society in which men control the major sources of power.

Patrilineal: links between kin are determined by the male line.

Patrilocal Residence: a wife moves into her husband's house after marriage.

Polygamy: a marriage rule allowing more than one spouse.

Polyandry: one wife with more than one husband.

Polygyny: one husband with more than one wife.

Romantic Love: strong sentiments of attachment and affiliation that bind together two individuals; an intimate sexual and emotional relationship between two individuals.

Samba: a dance form with African origins performed by samba schools during Carnival in Brazil

Sex: the biological categories of male, female, and intersex.

Sharia Law: official Islamic law.

Transgender: an umbrella term for people whose gender identity and/or gender expression differs from what is associated with the sex they were assigned at birth.

Transsexual (in Euro-American culture): a person who undergoes surgical and/or hormonal treatments to become a full member of their opposite biological sex.

References

Abu-Lughod, Lila. 1999/1986. *Veiled Sentiments: Honor and Poetry in a Bedouin Society.* Berkeley, CA: University of California Press.

———. 2017. "Is there a Muslim sexuality?: Changing Constructions of Sexuality in Egyptian Bedouin Weddings." In *Gender in Cross-Cultural Perspective*, 7th ed., edited by Caroline B. Brettell and Carolyn F. Sargent. New York: Routledge.

Ackroyd, Peter. 2018. *Queer City: Gay London from the Romans to the Present Day.* New York: Abrams Press.

Ahmed, Shaad. 2009, December 14. "Hadiths: The Marriage Process in Islam." icna.org./hadiths-the-marriage-process-in-islam/

Alfarah, Ziad, Fadi H. Ramaden, Emily Cury, and Gary H. Brandeis. 2012. "Muslim Nursing Homes in the United States: Barriers and Prospects." *Journal of Post-Acute and Long-Term Care Medicine* 13, no. 2: 176–179

Alloula, Malek. 1986. *The Colonial Harem.* Minneapolis, MN: University of Minnesota Press.

al-Sharif, Manal. 2017. *Daring to Drive: A Saudi Woman's Awakening.* New York: Simon & Schuster.

Banks, Ralph Richard. 2011. *Is Marriage for White People: How the African American Marriage Decline Affects Everyone.* New York: Dutton.

Barbara, Vanessa. 2017. "How I Learned to Yell." *New York Times*, November 12, SR9.

Barry, Brittany N. 2016. "Gender Roots: Conceptualizing 'Honor' Killing and Interpretation of Women's Gender in Muslim Society." *The Cupola*. https://cupola.gettysburg.edu/cgi/viewcontent.cgi?referer=https://www.google.com/&httpsredir=1&article=1001&context=islamandwomen

Bengali, Shashank, and Ramin Mostaghim. 2016. "More Women in Iran Are Forgoing Marriage. One Reason? The Men Aren't Good Enough." *Los Angeles Times*, November 11. http://www.latimes.com/world/la-fg-iran-unmarried-snap-story.html

Besnier, Niko. 2018. "Gender and Sexuality: Contested Relations." In *The International Encyclopedia of Anthropology*, edited by Hilary Callan, 1–7. New York: Wiley.

Blackwood, Evelyn. 2000. *Webs of Power: Women, Kin, and Community in a Sumatran Village.* New York: Rowman & Littlefield.

Blackwood, Evelyn, and Saskia E. Wieringa. 1999. *Female Desires: Same-sex Relations and Transgender Practices across Cultures.* New York: Columbia University Press.

Bolin, Anne. 1993. "Transcending and Transgendering: Male-to-Female Transsexuals, Dichotomy and Diversity." In *Third Sex, Third Gender: Beyond Sexual Dimorphism in Culture and History*, edited by Gilbert Herdt. New York: Zone Books.

Bowman, Karyln. 2018. "Is Premarital Sex Wicked? Changing Attitudes about Morality." *Forbes*, January 3. https//www.forbes.com/sites/bowmanmarsico/2018/01.03/is-premarital-sex-wicked-changing-attitudes-about-morality/

Breiding, M. C., J. Chen, and M. C. Black. 2014. *Intimate Partner Violence in the United States—2010*. Atlanta: National Center for Injury Prevention and Control, Centers for Disease Control.

Brettell, Caroline B., and Carolyn F. Sargent. 2017. *Gender in Cross-Cultural Perspective.* 7th ed. New York: Routledge.

Bride Wanted. 2018, June 24. Tribuneindia.com/news/classified-advts/brides-wanted/609656.html.

Burton, Richard, trans. 1962. *The Kama Sutra of Vatsyayana*. New York: E. P. Dutton.

Carneiro, Robert. 1981. "The Chiefdom: Precursor of the State." In *The Transition to Statehood in the New World*, edited by Grant Jones and Robert Kautz, 37–39. Cambridge, UK: Cambridge University Press.

Cassidy, Margaret L., and Gary R. Lee. 1989. "The Study of Polyandry: A Critique and a Synthesis." *Journal of Comparative Family Studies* 20, no. 1 (Spring): 1–11.

Chan, Selina Ching. 2006. "Love and Jewelry: Patriarchal Control, Conjugal Ties, and Changing Identities." In *Modern Loves: The Anthropology of Romantic Courtship and Companionate Marriage*, edited by Jennifer S. Hirsch and Holly Wardlow, 35–50. Ann Arbor: University of Michigan Press.

Charrad, Mounira M. 2001. *States and Women's Rights: The Making of Postcolonial Tunisia, Algeria, and Morocco.* Berkeley, CA: University of California Press.

Cherlin, Andrew J. 2014. "The Real Reason Richer People Marry." *New York Times*, December 7, SR3.

Childs, Geoff. 2003. "Polyandry and Population Growth in a Historical Tibetan Society." *History of the Family* 8: 423–444.

Childs, Geoff, Melvyn C. Goldstein, and Puchung Wangdui. 2011. "What to Do with Unmarried Daughters? Modern Solutions to a Traditional Dilemma in a Polyandrous Tibetan Society." *Journal of Cross-Cultural Gerontology* 26, no. 1: 1–22.

Ching, Frank. 2009. *Ancestors: 900 Years in the Life of a Chinese Family.* London: Penguin Random House.

Clemetson, Lynette. 2006. "U.S. Muslims Confront Taboo on Nursing Homes." *New York Times*, June 13, A1.

Cole, Jennifer, and Lynn M. Thomas. 2009. *Love in Africa*. Chicago: University of Chicago Press.

Coontz, Stephanie. 2005. *Marriage, a History: From Obedience to Intimacy or How Love Conquered Marriage.* New York: Viking.

Danielsson, Bengt. 1956. *Love in the South Seas.* New York: Reynal.

Davis, Douglas A., and Susan Schaefer Davis. 1995. "Possessed by Love: Gender and Romance in Morocco." www.haverford.edu/psychology/ddavis/romance.html

DeParle, Jason. 2012. "Two Classes, Divided by 'I Do': Marriage for Richer; Single Motherhood for Poorer." *New York Times*, July 15, A7.

Dettwyler, Katherine A. 2011. *Cultural Anthropology & Human Experience*. Long Grove, IL: Waveland Press.

Divakaruni, Chitra Banerjee. 1995. *Arranged Marriage: Stories*. New York: Doubleday/Anchor.

Donner, Henrike, ed. 2009. *Domestic Goddesses: Maternity, Globalization and Middle-Class Identity in Contemporary India*. New York: Routledge.

———. 2016. "Doing It Our Way: Love and Marriage in Kolkata Middle-Class Families." *Love, Marriage, and Intimate Citizenship in Contemporary China and India. Modern Asian Studies* 50 (4): 1147–1189.

Donner, Henrike, and Goncalo Santos. 2016. "Love, Marriage, and Intimate Citizenship in Contemporary China and India: An Introduction." *Modern Asian Studies* 50, no. 4: 1123–1146.

Dwyer, Rachel. 2000. *All You Want Is Money, All You Need Is Love: Sexuality and Romance in Modern India.* New York: Cassell.

Ebrey, Patricia Buckley. 1990. "Women, Marriage, and the Family in Chinese History." In *Heritage of China; Contemporary Perspectives on Chinese Civilization*, edited by Paul S. Ropp, 197–223. Berkeley: University of California Press.

Economist, The. 2011. "The Flight from Marriage," August 20.

El Feki, Shereen. 2013. *Sex and the Citadel: Intimate Life in a Changing Arab World.* New York: Pantheon.

Elfira, Mina. 2009. "'Not Muslim, Not Minangkabau': Interreligious Marriage and Its Cultural Impact in Minangkabau Society." In *Muslim-Non-Muslim Marriage: Political and Cultural Contestation in Southeast Asia*, edited by Gavin W. Jones, Chee Heng Leng, and Maznah Mohamad. Singapore: Institute of Southeast Asian Studies.

El Saadawi, Nawal. 2007. *The Hidden Face of Eve: Women in the Arab World.* London: Zed Books.

Erdbrink, Thomas. 2018. "Compulsory Veils? Half of Iranians Say 'No' to a Pillar of the Revolution." *New York Times*, February 5, A10.

"European Sex Attitudes versus American Sex Attitudes." 2010, November 16. *TeenNow California.* https://tnca.wordpress.com/2010/11/16/european-sex-attitudes-versus-american-sex-attitudes/

Farrer, James. 2002. *Opening Up: Youth Sex Culture and Market Reform in Shanghai.* Chicago: University of Chicago Press.

Feinberg, Richard. 1988. "Margaret Mead and Samoa: Coming of Age in Fact and Fiction." *American* Anthropologist 90, no. 3: 656–663.

Feinberg, Richard, and Cluny Macphersen. 2002. "Part II: The 'Eastern Pacific.'" In *Oceania: An Introduction to the Cultures and Identities of Pacific Islanders*, edited by Andrew Strathern, Pamela J. Stewart, Laurence M. Carucci, Lin Poyer, Richard Feinberg, and Cluny Macphersen, 100–179. Durham, NC: Carolina Academic Press.

Feldman, Douglas A., ed. 2008. *AIDS, Culture, and Africa.* Gainesville, University Press of Florida.

———, ed. 2010. *AIDS, Culture, and Gay Men. Africa.* Gainesville, University Press of Florida.

———. 2013. "Gay Marriage: The Struggle Is Far from Over." *Huffpost*, July 15. http://www.huffingtonpost.com/American-anthropological-association/gay-marriage-the-struggle-is-far-from_over_b_3573685.html

Fernea, Elizabeth W. 2003. "The Veiled Revolution." In *Everyday Life in the Muslim Middle East*, edited by Donna Lee Bowen and Evelyn A. Early, 119–122. Bloomington, IN: Indiana University Press.

Fillipi, Fillip de, ed. 1937. *An Account of Tibet: The Travels of Ippolito Desideri of Pistoria, S. J., 1712–1727.* London: Routledge and Sons.

Fisher, Helen. 2016. *Anatomy of Love: A Natural History of Mating, Marriage, and Why We Stray.* Rev. ed. New York: W. W. Norton.

Flock, Elizabeth. 2018. *The Heart Is a Shifting Sea: Love and Marriage in Mumbai.* New York: Harper.

FlorCruz, Michelle. 2015. "Dating Culture in China: Beijing's Single 'Leftover Women' and 'Bare Branch' Men Consider Forgoing Marriage." Ibtimes.com/dating-china-beijings-single-leftover-bare-branch-men-consider-forgoing-1816114

Ford, Peter. 2011. "'Naked Marriages' on Rise in China." *Christian Science Monitor*, November 11. https://www.csmonitor.com/World/Asia-Pacific/2011/1112/Naked-marriages-on-rise-in-China

Foucault, Michel. 1976. *The History of Sexuality. Volume 1: An Introduction.* New York: Vintage.

Freeman, Derek. 1983. *Margaret Mead and Samoa: The Making and Unmaking of an Anthropological Myth.* Cambridge, MA: Harvard University Press.
Gilmore, David D., ed. 1987. *Honor and Shame and the Unity of the Mediterranean.* Washington, DC: American Anthropological Association.
Gladstone, Rick. 2014. "Youths in 'Happy' Video Find Iran's Grip on Internet Is Still Tight." *New York Times*, May 21, A4. https://www.nytimes.com/2014/05/22/world/middleeast/arrests-after-dance-video-in-tehran-hint-at-cultural-war.html
Goldberg, Michelle. 2013. "Missing Girls." In *Annual Editions in Anthropology*, edited by Elvio Angeloni, 118–128. New York: McGraw Hill.
Goldstein, Donna M. 2013. *Laughter Out of Place: Race, Class, Violence, and Sexuality in a Rio Shantytown.* Berkeley: University of California Press.
Goldstein, Melvyn. 1976. "Fraternal Polyandry and Fertility in a High Himalayan Valley in Northwest Nepal." *Human Ecology* 4, no. 3: 223–233.
———. 1987. "When Brothers Share a Wife," *Natural History*, March, p. 39–49.
Goleman, Daniel. 1992. "After Kinship and Marriage, Anthropology Discovers Love." *New York Times*, November 24. https://www.nytimes.com/1992/11/24/science/after-kinship-and-marriage-anthropology-discovers-love.html
Gottleib, Alma. 2002. "Interpreting Gender and Sexuality: Approaches from Cultural Anthropology." In *Exotic No More: Anthropology on the Front Lines*, edited by Jeremy MacClancy, 167–189. Chicago: University of Chicago Press.
Gregg, Jessica. 2006. "'He Can Be Sad Like That': Liberdade and the Absence of Romantic Love in a Brazilian Shantytown." In *Modern Loves: The Anthropology of Romantic Courtship and Companionate* Marriage, edited by Jennifer S. Hirsch and Holly Wardlow, 157–171. Ann Arbor: University of Michigan Press.
Greenhalgh, Susan. 2007. "China's Future with Fewer Females." *China from the Inside.* Washington, DC: Public Broadcasting Service. www.pbs.org/kqed/chinainside/women/population.html
Grigoryeva, Angelina. 2017. "Own Gender, Sibling's Gender, Parent's Gender: The Division of Elderly Parent Care among Adult Children." *American Sociological Review* 82: 116–46.
Haack, Karla Rafaela, and Denise Falcke. 2014. "Love and Marital Quality in Romantic Relationships Mediated and Non-Mediated by Internet." *Paida: Sao Paulo* 24, no. 57: 105–113.
Hacker, Andrew. 2012. "We're More Unequal than You Think." *New York Review of Books*, February 23, 34
Harney, John. 2016. "How Do Sunni and Shia Islam Differ?" *New York Times*, January 3. https://www.nytimes.com/2016/01/04/world/middleeast/q-and-a-how-do-sunni-and-shia-islam-differ.html
Hautzinger, Sarah J. 2007. *Violence in the City of Women: Police and Batterers in Bahia, Brazil.* Berkeley: University of California Press.
Heilborn, M. L., and C. S. Cabral. 2013. "Youth, gender and sexual practices in Brazil." *Psicologia and Sociedade* 25: 33–43.
Hekma, Gert. 1993. "'A Female Soul in a Male Body': Sexual Inversion as Gender Inversion in Nineteenth-Century Sexology." In *Third Sex, Third Gender: Beyond Sexual Dimorphism in Culture and* Society, edited by Gilbert Herdt, 213–240. New York: Zone Books.
Herdt, Gilbert H. 1987. *The Sambia.* New York: Holt, Rinehart and Winston.
———, ed. 1993. *Third Sex, Third Gender: Beyond Sexual Dimorphism in Culture and History.* New York: Zone Books.
———. 1997. *Same Sex, Different Cultures: Exploring Gay and Lesbian Lives.* London: Routledge.
Hindert, Nicole Barreto. 2016. "The *Jeito* of the Brazilian Mulata: Race and Identity in a Racial Democracy." PhD Diss. Fairfax, VA: George Mason University. http://mars.gmu.edu/bitstream/handle/1920/10413/Hindert_gmu_0883E_11208.pdf?sequence=1&isAllowed=y

Hirsch, Jennifer S., and Holly Wardlow, eds. 2006. *Modern Loves: The Anthropology of Romantic Courtship and Companionate Marriage.* Ann Arbor: University of Michigan Press.

Hirsch, Jennifer S., Holly Wardlow, Daniel Jordan Smith, Harriet M. Phinney, Shanti Parikh, and Constance A. Nathanson, eds. 2009. *The Secret: Love, Marriage, and HIV.* Nashville, TN: Vanderbilt University Press.

Hitchcock, Amanda. 2001. "Rising Number of Dowry Deaths in India." *World Socialist Website.* https://www.wsws.org/en/articles/2001/07/ind-j04.html

Hossain, Adnan. 2012. "Beyond Emasculation: Being Muslim and Becoming Hijra in South Asia." *Asian Studies Review* 36, no. 4: 495–513.

Hua, Cai. 2001. *A Society without Fathers or Husbands: The Na of China.* New York: Zone Books.

Ickes, Scott. 2013. *African-Brazilian Culture and Regional Identity in Bahia, Brazil.* Gainesville: University of Florida Press.

Inhorn, Marcia C. 2007. "Loving Your Infertile Muslim Spouse: Notes on the Globalization of IVF and its Romantic Commitments in Sunni Egypt and Shia Lebanon." In *Love and Globalization: Transformations of Intimacy in the Contemporary World,* edited by Mark B. Padilla, Jennifer S. Hirsch, Miguel Munoz-Laboy, Robert E. Sember, and Richard G. Parkers, 139–160. Nashville, TN: Vanderbilt University Press.

Jankowiak, William. 2018. "When It Comes to Love, Is Three (or More) a Crowd?" *Sapiens,* February 14. https://www.sapiens.org/body/humans-monogamy-polyamory/

Jankowiak, William, and Edward F. Fischer. 1992. "A Cross Cultural Perspective on Romantic Love." *Ethnology* 31: 149–155.

Jankowiak, William, and Thomas Paladino. 2008. "Desiring Sex, Longing for Love: A Tripartite Conundrum." In *Intimacies: Love and Sex across Cultures,* edited by William Jankowiak, 1–36. New York: Columbia University Press.

Joans, Barbara. 2013. *The Changing Woman: Women of a Certain Age.* Amazon Publishing.

Jones, Gavin W. 2010. "Changing Marriage Patterns in Asia." *Asia Research Institute Working Paper Series 131.* http://www.ari.nus.edu.sg/wps/wps10_131.pdf

Kandiyoti, Deniz. 1988. "Bargaining with Patriarchy." *Gender and Society* 2 (3): 274–290.

Kapur, Cari Constanzo. 2010. "Rethinking Courtship, Marriage, and Divorce in an Indian Call Center." In *Everyday Life in South India,* 2nd ed., edited by Diane P. Mines and Sarah Lamb, 50–61. Bloomington: Indiana University Press.

Kenny, Mary. 2007. *Hidden Heads of Households: Child Labor in Urban Northeast Brazil.* Peterborough, Ontario: Broadview Press.

Khalaf, Samir, and Roseanne Saad Khalaf, eds. 2009. *Arab Society and Culture: An Essential Reader.* London: Saqi.

Kilbride, Philip L. 2006. "African Polygyny: Family Values and Contemporary Changes." In *Applying Cultural Anthropology: An Introductory Reader,* 5th ed., edited by Aaron Podolefsky and Peter J. Brown, 201–208. Mountain View, CA: Mayfield.

Kirk, Robert W. 2012. *Paradise Past: The Transformation of the South Pacific, 1520–1920.* Jefferson, NC: McFarland.

Klinenberg, Eric. 2012. *Going Solo: The Extraordinary Rise and Surprising Appeal of Living Alone.* New York: Penguin.

Knauft, Bruce. 2016. *The Gebusi: Lives Transformed in a Rainforest World.* 4th ed. Long Grove, IL: Waveland Press.

Kottak, Conrad. 2006. *Assault on Paradise: The Globalization of a Little Community in Brazil.* 4th ed. Long Grove, IL: Waveland Press.

Kramer, Sarah. 2011. "Three Generations under One Roof." *New York Times,* September 25, MB1.

Kreider, Rose M., and Renee Ellis. 2011. "Living Arrangements of Children: 2009." *Current Population Reports.* https://www.census.gov/prod/2011pubs/p70-126.pdf

Kristoff, Nicholas D., and Sheryl WuDunn. 2009. *Half the Sky: Turning Oppression into Opportunity for Women Worldwide.* New York: Alfred A. Knopf.

Kulick, Don. 1998. *Travesti: Sex, Gender and Culture among Brazilian Transgendered Prostitutes.* Chicago: University of Chicago Press.

Kunzig, Robert. 2011. "Population Seven Billion." *National Geographic*, January. https://www.nationalgeographic.com/magazine/2011/01/7-billion-population/

Lake, Roseann. 2018. *Leftover in China: The Women Shaping the World's Next Superpower.* New York: W.W. Norton.

Larmer, Brook. 2013. "The Price of Marriage in China." *New York Times*, March 9. nytimes.com/2013/03/10/business/in-a-changing-china-new-matchmaking-market.html

Lau, Tammy. 2017, April 13. What's the Average Age for Men and Women to Get Married? *Asia Wedding Network*. https://asiaweddingnetwork.com/en/magazine/expert-advice/1873-average-marriage-age-women-men-asia

Lenkeit, Roberta Edwards. 2019. *High Heels & Bound Feet: And Other Essays on Everyday Anthropology.* 2nd ed. Long Grove, IL: Waveland Press.

Lessinger, Johanna M. 2013. "Love and Marriage in the Shadow of the Sewing Machine: Case Studies from Chennai, India." In *Marrying in South Asia: Shifting Concepts, Changing Practises in a Globalizing* World, edited by Ravinder Kaur and Rajni Palriwalah, 234–252. Delhi: Orient Blackswan.

Levine, Nancy E. 1981 "Perspectives on Love: Morality and Affect in Nyinba Interpersonal Relationships." In *Culture and Morality: Essays in Honor of Christoph von Furer-Haimendorf*, edited by A. C. Meyer. Delhi: Oxford University Press.

———. 1988. *The Dynamics of Polyandry: Kinship, Domesticity, and Population on the Tibetan Border.* Chicago: University of Chicago Press.

Levine, Nancy E., and Joan B. Silk. 1997. "Why Polyandry Fails: Sources of Instability in Polyandrous Marriages." *Current Anthropology* 38, no. 3: 375–398. https://pdfs.semanticscholar.org/5a5a/f935b0c0c674050d3fb672a9cf8959654c82.pdf

Lévi-Strauss, Claude. 1969/1949. *The Elementary Structures of Kinship*. Boston: Beacon Press.

Li, Ma. n.d. "Cohabitation and Marriage in China: Past and Present." http://epc2016.princeton.edu/papers/160271

Lindstrom, Lamont. 2015. "Award-Winning Film *Tanna* Sets Romeo and Juliet in the South Pacific." *The Conversation*, November 4. http://theconversation.com/award-winning-film-tanna-sets-romeo-and-juliet-in-the-south-pacific-49874

Luker, Kristin. 1996. *Dubious Conceptions: The Politics of Teenage Pregnancy.* Cambridge, MA: Harvard University Press.

Lynch, Owen, ed. 1990. *Divine Passions: The Social Construction of Emotion in India.* Berkeley: University of California Press.

McFadden, Robert D. 2017. "Edith Windsor, Whose Same-Sex Marriage Fight Led to Landmark Ruling, Dies at 88." nytimes.com.2017/09/12/us/Edith-Windsor-dead-same-sex-marriage-doma.html

Mahdavi, Pardis. 2007. "Passionate Uprisings: Young People, Sexuality and Politics in Post-Revolutionary Iran." *Culture, Health & Sexuality* 9 no. 5: 445–457. https://pdfs.semanticscholar.org/7b44/a53e9f49dc18a4a7e7d103044d09eed9fe5c.pdf

———. 2009. *Passionate Uprisings: Iran's Sexual Revolution*. Redwood City, CA: Stanford University Press.

———. 2015. "Chastity." In *The International Encyclopedia of Human* Sexuality, edited by, Patricia Whelehan and Anne Bolin. New York: Wiley.

Mallozzi, Vincent M. 2018. "For Love of Country, and Each Other. *New York Times*, January 21, st 10.

Manji, Irshad. 2003. *The Trouble with Islam: A Wake-Up Call for Honesty and Change.* Toronto: Random House.

Mattison, Siobhan M., Bridget Chak, Hanying Mao, and Peter Buston. 2015. "Kinship and Sex-Biased Parental Investment among the Mosuo of Southwest China." *American Journal of Human Biology* 27, no. 2: 244–258.

Mattison, Siobhan M., Brooke Scelza, and Tami Blumenfield. 2014. "Paternal Investment and the Positive Effects of Fathers among the Matrilineal Mosuo of Southwest China." *American Anthropologist* 116, no. 3: 591–610.

Maxwell, Mary Beth. 2017. "Global LGBTQ Equality at a Crossroads." https://www.huffingtonpost.com/entry/global-lgbtq-equality-at-a-crossroads_us_5a2ee521e4b0cf10effbaf7f

Mazumdar, Shampa, and Sanjoy Mazumdar. 1999. "Ritual Lives of Muslim Women: Agency in Everyday Life." *Journal of Ritual Studies* 13, no. 2: 58–70.

Mead, Margaret. 1930. "The social organization of Manu'a." *Bernice P. Bishop Museum Bulletin* 76. Honolulu, HI: Bishop Museum.

———. 1973/1928. *Coming of Age in Samoa: A Psychological Study of Primitive Youth for Western Civilization.* New York: Morrow Quill Paperbacks.

Mernissi, Fatima. 2011. *Beyond the Veil: Male-Female Dynamics in Muslim Society.* London: Saqi.

Miller, Claire Cain. 2018. "A Baby Bust, Rooted in Economic Insecurity." *New York Times*, July 6, B5.

Miller, Claire Cain, and Liz Alderman. 2014. "The Flexibility Gap." *New York Times*, December 14, B1.

Miner, Horace. 2016/1956. "Body Ritual among the Nacirema." In *Distant Mirrors: America as a Foreign Culture*, 2nd ed., edited by Philip DeVita, 23–29. Long Grove, IL: Waveland Press.

Musallam, B. F. 1983. *Sex and Society in Islam.* Cambridge: Cambridge University Press.

Nakamatsu, Tomoko. 2011. "No Love, No Happy Ending?: The Place of Romantic Love in the Marriage Business and Brokered Cross-Cultural Marriages." In *International Marriages in the Time of Globalization*, edited by Elli K. Heikkila and Brenda S. A. Yeoh, 19–34. New York: Nova Science.

Nanda, Serena. 1983. "Voluntary Associations among Upper Middle-Class Women in Bombay." In *Urban India*, edited by Giri Raj Gupta, 299–324. New Delhi: Vikas

———. 1998. "Marriage and Kinship in (North) India." *American Anthropological Association; General Anthropology Division Modules in Teaching Anthropology.* Arlington, VA: American Anthropological Association.

———. 1999. *The Hijras of India: Neither Man nor Woman.* 2nd ed. Belmont, CA: Wadsworth.

———. 2014. *Gender Diversity: Crosscultural Variations.* 2nd ed. Long Grove, IL: Waveland Press.

———. 2016. "Arranging a Marriage in India." In *Distant Mirrors: America as a Foreign Culture*, 4th ed, edited by Philip R. DeVita, 124–135. Long Grove, IL: Waveland Press.

Nanda, Serena, and Joan Gregg. 2009. *The Gift of a Bride: A Tale of Anthropology, Matrimony and Murder.* New York: Roman and Littlefield/Altamira.

Nanda, Serena, and Richard L. Warms. 2018. *Culture Counts: A Concise Introduction to Cultural Anthropology.* 4th ed. Boston, MA: Cengage Learning.

National Center for Health Statistics. 2018. "Percentage of Births to Unmarried Mothers by State." Atlanta, GA: Centers for Disease Control and Prevention. https://www.cdc.gov/nchs/pressroom/sosmap/unmarried/unmarried.htm

Neuhouser, Kevin. 1989. "Sources of Women's Power and Status among the Urban Poor in Contemporary Brazil." *Signs* 14, no. 3 (Spring): 685–702.

New Straits Times. 2017. "Indonesia Court Rejects Bid to Outlaw Extramarital Sex." https://www.nst.com.my/world/2017/12/314646/indonesia-court-rejects-bid-outlaw-extramarital-sex

Newton, Esther. 1979. *Mother Camp: Female Impersonators in America.* Chicago: University of Chicago Press.

Nolen, Stephanie. 2015. "Black Is Beautiful, but White—White Is Just Easier." *Globe and Mail*, August 1, 1F.

Norgren, Jill, and Serena Nanda. 2006. *American Cultural Pluralism and Law.* 3rd ed. Westport, CT: Praeger.

Nyimba. 1992. *Cultural Survival Quarterly Magazine*. Cambridge, MA: Cultural Survival, Inc. https://www.culturalsurvival.org/publications/cultural-survival-quarterly/nyimba

Obendiek, Helena. 2016. "Rural Family Backgrounds, Higher Education, and Marriage Negotiations in Northwest China." *Modern Asian Studies* 50, no. 4: 1123–1146.

Ortner, Sherry B. 1981. "Gender and sexuality in hierarchical societies: the case of Polynesia and some comparative implications." In *Sexual Meanings: The Cultural Construction of Gender and Sexuality*, edited by Sherry B. Ortner and Harriet Whitehead, 359–409. Cambridge, UK: Cambridge University Press.

Pappu, Sridhar. 2017. "Love and Marriage, South Asian-American Style." *New York Times News Service.* Reprinted in *Little India,* Nov. 2017, p. 18.

Parker, Richard G. 2009. *Bodies, Pleasures, and Passions: Sexual Culture in Contemporary Brazil*. 2nd ed. Boston: Beacon.

Parenting in America. 2015. *Pew Social Trends.* www.pewsocialtrends.org/2015/12/17/1-the-american-family-today/

Posner, Sarah. 2018. "Cake-Case Concerns." *The Nation*, July 2/9, 4.

Qin, Amy. 2015. "'Kingdom of Daughters' Draws Tourists to Its Matrilineal Society." *New York Times*, October 26, A4.

Rabinowitz, Nancy Sorkin, and Lisa Auanger, eds. 2008. *Among Women: From the Homosocial to the Homoerotic in the Ancient World*. Austin: University of Texas Press.

Rebhun, L. A. 1999a. *The Heart Is Unknown Country.* Redwood City, CA: Stanford University Press.

———. 1999b. "For Love and for Money: Romance in Urbanizing Northeast Brazil." *City and Society* 11, no. 1–2 (June): 145–164.

Reddy, Gayatri. 2005. *With Respect to Sex: Negotiating Hijra Identity in South Asia*. Chicago: University of Chicago Press.

———. 2006. "The Bonds of Love: Companionate Marriage and the Desire for Intimacy among Hijras in Hyderabad, India." In *Modern Loves: The Anthropology of Romantic Courtship and Companionate Marriage*, edited by Jennifer S. Hirsch and Holly Wardlow, 174–192. Ann Arbor: University of Michigan Press.

Rind, Patricia. 2015. "Gender Identity and Role." In *The Encyclopedia of Sexuality*, edited by Patricia Whelehan and Anne Bolin. New York: Wiley.

Roscoe, Will. 1998. *Changing Ones: Third and Fourth Genders in Native North America*. London: Macmillan.

Rubin, Alissa J. 2016. "Penalizing Women for Covering Too Little, and Then Too Much." *New York Times*, August 28, N5.

Sanday, Peggy Reeves. 2002. *Women at the Center: Life in a Modern Matriarchy.* Ithaca, NY: Cornell University Press.

Sandhya, Shaifali. 2009. *Love Will Follow: Why the Indian Marriage Is Burning*. Noida, India: Random House.

Santos, Goncalco. 2016. "On Intimate Choices and Troubles in Rural South China." *Modern Asian* Studies, 50, no. 4: 1298–1326.

Scheper-Hughes, Nancy. 1993. *Death without Weeping: The Violence of Everyday Life in Brazil.* Berkeley: University of California Press

———. 2013. "No More Angel Babies on the Alto." *Center for Latin American Studies.* clas.berkeley.edu/research/brazil-no-more-angel-babies-alto

Seth, Vikram. 1993. *A Suitable Boy.* United States: HarperCollins.

Shankman, Paul. 1996. "The History of Samoan Sexual Conduct and the Mead-Freeman Controversy." *American Anthropologist* 98, no. 3: 555–567.

———. 2009. *The Thrashing of Margaret Mead: Anatomy of an Anthropological Controversy.* Madison: WI: University of Wisconsin Press.

———. 2013. "The Fateful Hoaxing of Margaret Mead: A Cautionary Tale." *Current Anthropology* 54, no. 1: 51–70.

Shore, Bradd. 1981. "Sexuality and Gender in Samoa: Conceptions and Missed Conceptions." In *Sexual Meanings: The Cultural Construction of Gender and Sexuality,* edited by Sherry B. Ortner and Harriet Whitehead, 167–192. Cambridge: Cambridge University Press.

Shostak, Marjorie. 1981. *The !Kung of Nyae Nyae.* Cambridge, MA: Harvard University Press.

Siamdoust, Nahid. 2018. "Hanging Up Their Head Scarves." *New York Times.* February 6, A21. https://www.nytimes.com/2018/02/03/opinion/sunday/iran-hijab-women-scarves.html

Sims, Shannon. 2018. "Rhythm of the Streets: 'We're Warrior Women, and Yes, We Can Play.'" *New York Times*, February 6, A5.

Skidmore, Thomas E. 2009. *Brazil: Five Centuries of Change.* 2nd ed. New York: Oxford University Press.

Smith, Daniel Jordan. 2001. "Romance, Parenthood, and Gender in a Modern African Society." *Ethnology* 40, no. 2: 129–151.

———. 2006. "Love and the Risk of HIV." In *Modern Loves: The Anthropology of Romantic Courtship and Companionate Marriage*, edited by Jennifer S. Hirsch and Holly Wardlow. Ann Arbor: University of Michigan Press.

———. 2009a. "Managing Men, Marriage, and Modern Love: Women's Perspectives on Intimacy and Male Infidelity in Southeastern Nigeria. In *Love in* Africa, edited by Jennifer Cole and Lynn M. Thomas, 157–180. Chicago: University of Chicago Press.

———. 2009b. "Gender Inequality, Infidelity and the Social Risks of Modern Marriage in Nigeria." In *The Secret: Love, Marriage and HIV*, edited by editors Jennifer Hirsch, Holly Wardlow, Daniel Jordan Smith, Harriet M. Phinney, Shanti Parikh, and Constance Nathanson, 84–107. Nashville, TN: Vanderbilt University Press.

———. 2017. *To Be a Man Is Not a One-Day Job: Masculinity, Money, and Intimacy in Nigeria.* Chicago: University of Chicago Press.

Sokolofsky, Jay. 2009. *The Cultural Contexts of Aging.* 3rd ed. Westport, CT: Praeger.

Stampler, Laura. 2014. "How China's Singles' Day Holiday Sold Out." *Time*, November 11. http://time.com/3576381/china-singles-day-history/

Stockard, Janice E. 2002. *Marriage in Culture: Practice and Meaning across Diverse Societies.* Belmont, CA: Wadsworth, Cengage.

Sullivan, Gerald, and Sharon W. Tiffany. 2009. "The Gang of Four: Gregory Bateson, Ruth Benedict, Reo Fortune, and Margaret Mead in Multiple Contexts." *Pacific Studies* 32, nos. 2/3 (June/Sept): 131–392.

Tavernise, Sabrina. 2008. "Putting a Dent in a Law against Insulting Turkishness." *New York Times*, January 25, A4.

Thomas, Lynn M., and Jennifer Cole. 2009. "Thinking through Love in Africa." In *Love in Africa*, edited by Jennifer Cole and Lynn M. Thomas, 1–30. Chicago: University of Chicago Press.

Tiffany, Sharon W. 2009. "Narrative, Voice, and Genre in Margaret Mead's Coming of Age in Samoa." *Pacific Studies* 32, nos. 2/3 (June/Sept): 163–201.

Tiwari, Geetanjali. 2008. "Interplay of Love, Sex, and Marriage in a Polyandrous Society in the High Himalayas of India." In *Intimacies: Love and Sex Across Cultures*, edited by William R. Jankowiak, 122–147. New York: Columbia University Press.

Trivedi, Ira. 2014. *India in Love: Marriage and Sexuality in the 21st Century.* New Delhi: Aleph Book Company.

Trumbach, Randolph. 1993. "London's Sapphists: From Three Sexes to Four Genders in the Making of Modern Culture." In *Third Sex, Third Gender*, edited by Gilbert Herdt, 111–136. New York: Zone Books.

van der Meer, Theo. 1993. "Sodomy and the Pursuit of a Third Sex in the Early Modern Period." In *Third Sex, Third* Gender, edited by Gilbert Herdt, 137–212. New York: Zone Books.

Wang, Pan. "How TV Dating Shows Helped Change Love and Marriage in China Forever." Theconversation.com/how-tv-dating-shows-helped-change-love-and-marriage-forever-60594.

Wardlow, Holly. 2006. "All's Fair When Love Is War: Romantic Passion and Companionate Marriage among the Huli of Papua New Guinea." In *Modern Loves: The Anthropology of Romantic Courtship and Companionate Marriage*, edited by Jennifer S. Hirsch and Holly Wardlow, 51–77. Ann Arbor: University of Michigan Press.

Wee, Sui-Lee. 2017. "In China, Guys Enroll in Dating 101." *New York Times*, November 19, B1.

Westermarck, E. 1925. *The History of Human Marriage*. London: Macmillan.

Whitehouse, Bruce. 2018. "The Exaggerated Demise of Polygyny: Transformations in Marriage and Gender Relations in West Africa." In *International Handbook on Gender and Demographic Processes*, edited by Nancy Riley and Jan Brunson, 299–313. Dordrecht: Springer.

Wieringa, Saskia E. 2007. "'If there is no feeling . . .' The Dilemma between Silence and Coming Out in a Working-Class Butch/Femme Community in Jakarta." In *Love and Globalization: Transformations of Intimacy in the Contemporary* World, edited by Mark B. Padilla et al., 69–89. Nashville, TN. Vanderbilt University Press.

Wikan, Unni. 2008. *In Honor of Fadime: Murder and Shame*. Chicago: University of Chicago Press.

Wildsmith, Elizabeth, Nicole R. Steward-Streng, and Jennifer Manlove. 2011. "Childbearing Outside of Marriage: Estimates and Trends in the United States." *Child Trends Research Brief*, No. 2011–29. https://www.childtrends.org/wp-content/uploads/02/Child_Trends-2011_11_01_RB_NonmaritalCB.pdf

Willett, Jeff. 1997. "Tibetan Fraternal Polyandry: A Review of its Advantages and Breakdown." *Nebraska Anthropologist* 113. http://digitalcommons.unl.edu/nebanthro/113

Winter, Sam. 2015. "Transgender." In *The Encyclopedia of Sexuality*, edited by Patricia Whelehan and Anne Bolin. New York: Wiley.

Xinxin, Zhang, and Sang Ye. 1987. *Chinese Lives: An Oral History of Contemporary China*. New York: Pantheon.

Yamada, Masahiro. 2017. "Decline of Real Love and Rise of Virtual Love: Love in Asia." *International Journal of Japanese* Sociology, no. 26: 6–12. https://onlinelibrary.wiley.com/doi/pdf/10.1111/ijjs.12066

Zavoretti, Roberta. 2016. "Is It Better to Cry in a BMW or to Laugh on a Bicycle? Marriage, 'Financial Performance Anxiety,' and the Production of Class in Nanjing, People's Republic of China." *Modern Asian Studies* 50, no. 4: 1190–1219.

Zhi, Qu. 2014, March 6. "Flash: It's No Longer till Death Do Us Part. *ShanghaiDaily.com*. https://archive.shine.cn/archive/metro/in-depth/Flash-Its-no-longer-till-death-do-us-part/shdaily.shtml

Zoepf, Katherine. 2008. "In Booming Gulf, Some Arab Women Find Freedom in the Skies." *New York Times*, December 21, A1.

———. 2016. *Excellent Daughters: The Secret Lives of Young Women Who Are Transforming the Arab World*. New York: Penguin.

Index